YOSEMITE
STORIES UNTOLD

Yosemite: Stories Untold is published under Catharsis, a sectionalized division under Di Angelo Publications, Inc.

Catharsis is an imprint of Di Angelo Publications.
Copyright 2025.
All rights reserved.
Printed in the United States of America.

Di Angelo Publications
Los Angeles, California

Library of Congress
Yosemite: Stories Untold
ISBN: 978-1-962603-21-8
Hardback

Compiler: John Long
Cover Design: Savina Deianova
Interior Design: Kimberly James
Editor: Willy Rowberry

Downloadable via www.dapbooks.shop and other e-book retailers

No part of this publication may be reproduced, distributed, or transmitted in any form or by any means without the prior written permission of the publisher, except in the case of brief quotations embodied in critical reviews and certain other noncommercial uses permitted by copyright law. For permission requests, contact info@diangelopublications.com.

For educational, business, and bulk orders, contact sales@diangelopublications.com.

1. Literary Collections --- Subjects & Themes --- Places
2. Sports & Recreation --- Rock Climbing
3. Biography & Autobiography --- Memoirs

YOSEMITE
STORIES UNTOLD

AN ANTHOLOGY COMPILED BY
JOHN LONG

CONTENTS

INTRODUCTION — 11
John Long

SOME YOSEMITE ROCK CLIMBS — 17
William Shand, Jr.; *American Alpine Journal*

FIVE DAYS AND NIGHTS ON THE LOST ARROW — 27
Anton Nelson, *Sierra Club Bulletin*

ORDEAL BY PITON — 33
Allen Steck, *Sierra Club Bulletin*

THE NORTHWEST FACE OF HALF DOME — 41
Michael P. Sherrick, *Sierra Club Bulletin*

THE LONGEST CLIMB — 50
Wayne Merry, *Yosemite in the Fifties*

THE NORTH AMERICAN WALL — 66
Royal Robbins, *American Alpine Journal*

THE SOUTH FACE OF MT. WATKINS — 74
Chuck Pratt, *American Alpine Journal*

TIS-SA-ACK — 88
Royal Robbins, *Ascent*

TEAM MACHINE (1976) — 102
Billy Westbay, *The Valley Climbers*

THE LAST PITCH (1976) 106
John Long, *The Valley Climbers*

EL CAP AND HALF DOME IN A DAY 113
Peter Croft, *The Valley Climbers*

THE SALATHÉ FREE 119
Paul Piana, *American Alpine Journal*

FREEING THE NOSE IN ONE DAY (1994) 126
Lynn Hill, *The Valley Climbers*

SOLOING THE LINK-UP (1998) 135
Hans Florine, *The Valley Climbers*

EL NIÑO: FREEING THE NORTH AMERICAN WALL (1998) 141
Thomas Huber, *The Valley Climbers*

LURKING FEAR (2000) 148
Beth Rodden, *The Valley Climbers*

EL CORAZÓN! (2001) 159
Alexander Huber, *The Valley Climbers*

FREE RIDER IN A DAY (2004) 162
Steph Davis, *The Valley Climbers*

THE DIHEDRAL WALL (2004) 168
Tommy Caldwell, *The Valley Climbers*

LOSING MYSELF ON HALF DOME (2008) 179
Alex Honnold, *The Valley Climbers*

SPEED TRAP (2021) 188
John Long, *Ascent*

**MAGIC MUSHROOM: A FEMALE ASCENT OF EL
CAP'S SECOND-HARDEST FREE ROUTE (2017)** 213
Barbara Zangerl, *American Alpine Journal*

EL NIÑO VIA PINEAPPLE EXPRESS — GROUND UP. FREE. 218
Amity Warme (2024)

INTRODUCTION

John Long

Big Rock is a small, scrappy climbing area in Southern California. Technical climbing first came to the crag in the late 1940s, when soldiers from nearby March Air Force Base sieged the water-trough running up the middle of the 150-foot-high face. Throughout the 1950s and '60s, Big Rock was one of several training grounds for the RCS (Rock Climbing Section of the Sierra Club) and the Riverside Mountain

Rescue Team. Meanwhile, generations of Los Angeles- and San Diego-based climbers arrived by the van-load and clambered over every inch of the smooth diorite slab, bringing the business. Big Rock's Golden Age occurred in the mid-to-late 1960s, when Lee Harrel, Paul and Phil Gleason, Pat Callis, Charlie Raymond, Phil Haney, Keith Leaman, John Gosling, and a few others pushed the limits of slab climbing in the old, hard-rubber-soled shoes.

Just as my generation entered high school and began learning the ropes (circa 1971), authorities closed down Big Rock as construction began on a nearby dam and reservoir project, comprising the Perris Lake Recreation

Area. So my generation never overlapped with the old guard who established all those exciting climbs, suddenly abandoned. When we started sneaking onto Big Rock, as an army of workers built out the dam and reservoir, the place felt like a lost wing of the Smithsonian. We were anxious to follow the chalk marks of the caste of Big Rock veterans who had dominated Southern California climbing for over a decade.

How had this entire generation of SoCal pioneers just up and vanished? What had gone on here at Big Rock? We had to find out.

We started parking out on the highway, half a mile away from Big Rock, and sneaking in. We were well clear of the workers, derricks, and skip loaders, so by the time a foreman was bothered to chase us off, we had usually scaled a handful of routes and were good to go. When the same cranky boss kept catching us, we started leaving a half pint of Old Forester on the boulder near the base of the slab. Then we were free to climb all day—no questions asked. These were simpler times.

Once the dam was completed, they reopened Big Rock to climbing, and for the last thirty-five years, countless SoCal climbers have learned the ropes there. But our glory days out at Big Rock were when we first visited the place and seemed to have it all to ourselves, knowing we were using the footholds of the climbers whose names were strewn across guidebook pages of all the local crags. They were gone now and there was nothing but rusty quarter-inch Rawl Drive expansion bolts, widely spaced, to suggest that here at Big Rock, they had smoked their

Marlboros, ate baloney sandwiches on white bread, and took huge skidding falls, if the rumors were true. Legend says they took pictures of each other with Keith Leaman's Kodak Brownie, stuffed in a gym sock crammed inside a Folgers Coffee can. But no one ever saw a single photograph. Only their routes remained, proof that they'd mastered small hold and friction climbing and learned how to engineer face climbs. Back in the day.

It felt like boarding a time machine when throw-back articles started appearing on Supertopo.com about Big Rock's salad days.

"Just mention Big Rock and my fingertips burn and my calves tighten," wrote Phil Gleason, who along with his brother Paul, were central figures in the 1960s Big Rock zeitgeist. "I can still feel the excitement we used feel when driving up and first seeing its 'huge' bald face. I remember the sweet-sage, desert-rock smell after a rainstorm. Our first taste of the addicting intoxicants of adventure, and the warmth and magic of climber camaraderie. Wandering around the place in a happy little band, discovering and working on boulder problems till one, then the rest of the group unlocked the mystery. We were famous to each other, back when thrills were cheap, laughter came easily, and pleasure was as simple as the sun coming over that dome of rock and warming the chilled belayer."

Big Rock was but a brief aside of the much larger drama we all eventually acted out in Yosemite and beyond. Much as we had longed for some written history about Big Rock, there were scads of articles about climbing in

Yosemite, "the Mecca of world rock climbing," then and now. And of course we feasted on books and articles about the bold adventures of Yosemite big wall pioneer, John Salathea, followed by the seminal routes pioneered in the late 1950s and 1960s by Warren Harding, Royal Robbins, et al, when many of the world's most iconic and sought-after rock climbs were first established. But I'm getting ahead of myself. The strange thing—though it usually works this way for one and all—is that the moment my generation started creeping above the high-water mark set by the Yosemite pioneers, Yosemite climbing history became irrelevant to us. All that mattered, to ourselves and the reading public—as we watched the popularity of climbing detonate like an atom bomb—is what was happening NOW.

It has to work that way for every generation to make their mark and nudge the bar higher. However, somewhere in the 1990s, sport climbing took the adventure in such a new direction that the past was no longer a living history, whereby every generation was tied into the same rope, so to speak. Rather, the past was largely forgotten and only the present had ever existed. The extent that this had transpired was driven home to me in 2015 when Tommy Caldwell and Kevin Jorgesen's "heroic 19-day battle for the first free ascent of The Dawn Wall, which represented a monumental milestone in the climbing history books." Widely considered the hardest big wall in the world.

I was then an ambassador for a popular outdoor clothing brand that was also Kevin's main sponsor. This was the biggest media event in the history of adventure sports, and mobile news trucks lined the road running along the fringe of El Cap meadow, which for nearly three-weeks teamed with hundreds of spectators. Much to my surprise, when spectators—including many leading climbers—were asked about Golden Age Yosemite pioneers Warren Harding (who made the first ascent of the Dawn Wall in 1970), and Royal Robbins, who made the 2nd ascent, most admitted they only knew those names in passing. Yosemite Climbing history, in other words, was only now being recorded. Anything prior was meaningless.

I will not here argue that in one crucial way, we need to know the past to know ourselves. We also need to forget the past to discover what we might do. Yet we might have it both ways. Why bother? Read the following stories, that run the gamut from the first meaningful ascents in Yosemite, back in the 1940s, to the cutting-edge efforts of the last few years. Every climber in every one of those ascents were forced to deal with formidable obstacles in the here and now, but perhaps without knowing it, they were intimately connected to the past and the future because every rock climb is a wall of phantoms, when the past meets the present where the rubber meets the rock.

Unlike many other adventure sports, rock climbs are literally fixed in stone. The Salathea Wall that Royal Robbins, Chuck Pratt, and Tom Frost first climbed in 1961, is the selfsame wall Tod Skinner and Paul Piana free climbed in 1987, where speed climbers Jason Wells and Tim Klein died on in 2017, and where a yet unknown climber from the future will do without the rope for the first solo ascent.

Everyone in between will find themselves at a hanging belay high above the trees that every other ascent has used since the long lost first worked out a passage on the rock. Decades, perhaps even centuries later, at the juncture of back then and not yet, the young and fit will rope up for a route and climb it right now, riding old routes into the future, following the line of phantoms whose bones might well be dust. We are the same ghosts following the same holds, dangling side by side at the belay, paying out the memories. The collected astonishment, ingrained in the rock, murmurs to those still on their way, fearing yet craving their first lead.

Every climb is historical and every climber is a time-traveler because every crag is a haunted house. But there is only one Yosemite Valley.

SOME YOSEMITE ROCK CLIMBS

William Shand, Jr.
From the *American Alpine Journal*, 1944

Although nearly all the major summits of Yosemite had been ascended prior to 1900, it was not until 1934 that serious modern rock-climbing was undertaken in the valley. Since that time members of the Sierra Club of California have pioneered routes on faces and pinnacles comparable in difficulty with the best granite climbs of other regions of the world. Accounts of the earlier ascents, notably of the Cathedral Spires, earned for Yosemite a reputation expressed in a recent guidebook as a region characteristic of "rock-climbing of greatest difficulty, which can be undertaken only by experts."

It is true that many of the most popular routes are of fifth and sixth class difficulty, yet countless other climbs are to be found, from pleasant scrambles such as Grizzly Peak and Mt. Starr King to long climbs of intermediate difficulty such as Washington Column. Exceptionally competent women have climbed the Spires, although I believe that no woman has as yet led a Class Six climb in Yosemite. It might be mentioned, incidentally, that the first "Class Six" climb in the valley was accomplished in 1875, when George Anderson, the trailbuilder, engineered his way to the summit of Half Dome by drilling holes for eyebolts through which a rope was threaded along the line of the present "Cable Route." Like the ascent of Devils Tower in Wyoming, this feat was accomplished long before the advent of modern rock-climbing.

Although I had visited Yosemite in 1939, it was not until the following year that I was able to make any of the climbs in the valley. After first seeing the Cathedral Spires I was smitten by an overpowering desire to reach their summits — a feeling which is no doubt common in all climbers when they spy an apparently inaccessible and forbidding crag. The Cathedral Spires were the first of the difficult climbs in Yosemite to be accomplished. These slender pinnacles stand to the east of the Cathedral Rocks, towering 2,100 ft. above the valley floor. The original routes with minor variations are still the only ones completed, and they are still not "an easy day for a lady."

An hour of scrambling over talus and through the cool forest at the base of the terrifying N. faces brings one to the saddle connecting the Spires with the cliffs of the valley rim. From the saddle the foreshortened S. W. face of the higher Spire presents a much more broken appearance than from the road below, but a closer examination soon disillusions the optimist. Fortunately, we were not particularly optimistic that day since we had as usual slept late, and started later still. From the saddle a series of cracks and ledges leads upwards to the N. to "First Base," the wide ledge where the difficult climbing begins. There the lead devolved upon me, the others kindly declining this dubious honor on various pretenses of slight credibility.

After surmounting the initial overhang, one traverses on a perpendicular face around one of the most spectacular corners in the valley onto the "Bathtubs." These peculiar solution ledges are wide enough to balance on, but lack confidence — inspiring handholds above, and overhang the W. face, which plunges 500 ft. into the forest below. I experienced that unusual sensation which one might have on stepping out onto the sill of a window on the 50th floor of the Empire State Building, and preparing to climb around to the next window.

I kept up a conversation with Raffi Bedayan, who was belaying me, by means of an echo from the face of middle Cathedral Rock, since I was now out of sight around the corner, and the rope was running through the karabiners with considerable difficulty. The friction is considerably lessened by the use of two ropes, the one used through the karabiners up to the corner, when it is allowed to hang free and the second rope is snapped in. In spite of the expansion-bolt which protects the last part of the lead, a narrow crack above the "Bathtubs," I was happy to embrace the little tree at the top of the crack, and dangling one foot on each side of the trunk, spent the next half hour gazing down at the talus while the others apparently decided, one by one, not to do the higher Spire that day. Finally Bedayan appeared around the corner below, cheerfully remarking that the worst was over; we had at least made the first pitch.

In a few minutes we were at the base of the "Rotten Chimney," really a smooth open face of vertically fractured and rather unsound rock. Fortunately, most of the pitons were in place. There were 17 altogether, and since we only had 10 karabiners it was somewhat of a problem to decide which ones to ignore — except for the ones at the top of the overhang, which gave me a few nasty moments before I could struggle out onto the narrow platform to recover wind and confidence.

Bedayan followed in short order while I belayed from behind a convenient buttress of rock. At "Third Base," the ledge below the summit block, I took a look a look around the N. corner of the ledge while prospecting for the route, but unprepared for the terrifying view, recoiled with some profanity from the precipice which falls almost a 1,000 perpendicular feet to the base of the Spire. The old route ascended a piton ladder in a vertical crack in the S. W. face, but there are at least three easier variations. It might be remarked that for some time after the first ascents of the Spires and other routes, the climbers, fascinated by the fact that the ascents could be accomplished at all, seemed to ignore the possibility of safer and easier variations, and to specialize in lowering the speed records.

This situation now seems to have gone to the other extreme, and some of the climbs are in danger of being lowered by one class of difficulty. The variation we chose was certainly not difficult, though quite exposed. We traversed around the S. face of the summit block along a narrow ledge and ascended an easy crack to the spacious summit. On the highest point appeared the inevitable dwarf pine. A yodel of triumph brought a faint reply from far below on the saddle, where the others awaited our return.

The view from both the Spires is remarkable in that one feels that the summit rock must be floating in space; no ridges, no faces are visible from the tops. The view to the lower Spire is much like the view of the Winklerturm from the Stabelerturm in the Vajolet Group in the Dolomites. The shadows of the Cathedral Rocks, striding up the valley, warned us that we were late, and we hastened to descend. The scrub pine furnished an excellent roping-off point, and rappelling in 100-ft. pitches from tree to tree in the S. W. face to the right of the climbing route, we soon returned to "First Base." The last rappel, an 80-ft. overhang, leaves two alternatives: going slowly and getting dizzy from revolving, or going fast and burning off the rappel-patch. Having no patch, I preferred the former method, while Bedayan took the latter.

The lower Cathedral Spire is generally considered easier than the higher, although the "Flake" pitch is more difficult than any pitch on the higher Spire. Late in September 1941, Dave Lind, of the Seattle Mountaineers, and I reached the base of the lower Spire via the long curving talus slope to the E. of the Spires. While prospecting for the route we visited the notch between the Spires — a splendid gap which drops abruptly on the N. side to the forest far below, a viewpoint which should not be missed by climber or off-trail hiker. Since we knew that the first pitch was unusually severe, we started up the wrong place, and soon got into greater and greater difficulties. Descending, we started again higher up on the correct route, beneath a tree growing out under an overhang. Ants chased us up the chimney to "Main Ledge," but the traverse to the block beneath the "Flake" confused them, and we were pursued no more. I won the toss to see who would lead the "Lake," and being unable to persuade Lind that I was quite willing that he should do it, tied in to the double rope while he tied in to the pitons. A shoulder stand enabled me to grope around for holds that did not materialize, but somehow I got started on the face and reached what the Climbers' Guide calls an "almost inadequate ledge." I should like to delete the word "almost." A traverse to the left, up, and back to the right, and a few shakes later I was under the "Flake" itself.

This remarkable exfoliation slab is some 60 ft. high, a mere shell at the outer edge, and about 2 ft. thick at the base, a very precarious looking affair indeed. A loop of sling-rope is thrown over a projecting point on the lower corner of the "Flake" about 6 ft. beyond a one-inch ledge on which the climber stands in a perpendicular face some 30 ft. above the belayer, the rope trailing in a semicircle through the karabiners along the way. Once the loop catches, the difficulties are over, and the thin edge of the "Flake" is carefully surmounted. I never did quite understand how Lind got started off the block, but after a while his smiling face appeared over the edge of the "Flake" with the remark "Quite a drop-off here!"

The view from the ledge above the "Flake" gives one a remarkable impression of the steepness of the N. face of Sentinel Rock. Two variations are possible from the ledge, the earlier one considerably more difficult. We chose the easier way, traversing to the right along the ledge and up onto the corner of the E. face. In a couple of 100-ft. pitches we were on the summit, the W. end of which overhangs the N. W. face. After signing the register and dropping a pebble over the overhang we hastened to join some friends who were exploring the ravine behind the Spires. Roping down over the "Flake" was much more fun than climbing up it!

By far the most popular climb in Yosemite Valley, to judge from the number of ascents, is Washington Column. Standing at the eastern end of the Royal Arches, opposite Half Dome, this great mass of rock forms a giant cornerstone where Tenaya Canyon enters the valley. Most of the climb is four class in difficulty; one pitch on the usual route, the "Piton Traverse," is fifth class. In 1940 a "direct route" of greater difficulty was made, and later climbed in winter. Perhaps the route is popular because within five minutes of leaving the automobile, one can rope up and start an 1,800-ft. rock-climb! The length of the climb usually necessitates an early start — needless to say, our party was late in getting under way on Memorial Day, 1942, despite the threat of a bivouac on the Column. At the base of the chimney separating the Royal Arches from the Column one climbs into the face and follows a series of easy ledges and cracks for about 1000 ft. diagonally upwards to the E. to "Lunch Ledge," where the more difficult climbing begins. Actually lunch was consumed some distance below the ledge, since none of us had been on the route before, and we expected a much narrower ledge than it actually turned out to be. While eating we admired the impressive view of the Arches, with water raining from the overhang and drifting over to us with occasional gusts of wind. Across the valley we could see the route in the E. face of Glacier Point which we had climbed the previous autumn; now it was practically a waterfall.

Some distance higher we finally found the ice-pitons which mark "Lunch Ledge" and the beginning of the "Piton Traverse." Deciding to risk a bivouac, we started the traverse, a 75-ft. pitch on a 65° smooth, rounded face with minute, polished holds, a severe test of balance and friction. A 100 ft. beyond, a rope-traverse from an alcove gives access to the top of the chimney between the Arches and the Column, above where the stream pours over the great overhang to dissipate itself in spray far below. The chimney was wet, and full of damp and slippery moss and lichen. Using felt-soled Kletterschuhe which I had fortunately brought along, the upper waterfalls were climbed without serious difficulty, although not without discomfort; the rest slipped and slid up the rope through the water at the worst place. We emerged at the top at 6.30 p.m., and held a council to decide how to go down. Instead of roping down the Mirror Lake side, the usual procedure, we decided to hike down Indian Canyon by crossing over the Royal Arches. This sad underestimate of distance finally brought us to the head of Indian Creek shortly after dark, and forced a bivouac upon us. The alpenglow on the snowy High Sierras and the spectacle of the firefall from the Arches opposite Yosemite Point nearly recompensed that cold night on the valley rim.

In spite of the fact that nearly all the summits of Yosemite, with the exception of the Lost Arrow, have now been attained, countless fine climbs of all degrees of difficulty still remain to be made. The opportunities for route-finding on new faces is almost unlimited. Taft Arête, the N. face of Clouds Rest, the N. face of Sentinel Rock, Watkins Gulley, and many other routes are still unfinished. The problem which still fascinates most of the climbers is the Lost Arrow, the awe-inspiring needle on the cliffs to the east of Yosemite Falls. The summit has jokingly been called the "Last Error," the first three "Errors" being prominent ledges on the proposed route, the lower part of which has been ascended several times. The upper part has been reconnoitered by roping down from the valley rim. The ascent will probably be more difficult, from a technical point of view, than the most difficult climb yet made in the valley, the Arrowhead Chimney, a route which borders on the suicide climbs of the Wetterstein and the Kaisergebirge. It is to be hoped that the facts of Half Dome and El Capitan will never develop into American Eigerwands, but with due apology to Professor Whitney, I shall nevertheless not make the statement that they never will be climbed.

FIVE DAYS AND NIGHTS ON THE LOST ARROW

Anton Nelson

From the *Sierra Club Bulletin*, March 1948

What is required to climb Yosemite's Lost Arrow? For years many determined men had tried to find out just that. In trying they succeeded only in showing how terribly close to unclimbable the Arrow really is. Then, on September 3, 1947, John Salathé and I completed a successful assault, which we had begun 103 hours earlier at the base of the spire.

True, men had stood atop its summit one year before when a trip from the rim was ingeniously engineered by four Sierra Club climbers. Spectacular and effective though it was, this maneuver required very little real climbing; it was in effect an admission of the Arrow's unclimbability. The problem the Arrow poses for the climber is to ascend from the base up through the ramparts of the great chimney that cuts the spire away from the cliff, and past the three intermediate ledges, called Errors, until he reaches the summit, facetiously called the Fourth or Last Error.

Our basic idea was that we would climb safely or not at all. We understood that rescue from an accident in the Great Chimney was not to be expected. Bombproof belays were in order and unprotected leads of more than 10 or 15 feet were out of order. When the leader had to take a long chance he did so only when pitons (or bolts) that were sound enough for the anticipated fall were nearby and the belayer was on special alert. Then the most that could happen (and not infrequently did happen) was that the leader would take a controlled fall and go right back to work.

For climbing on the Arrow, great strength is far less important than patience and endurance. On the first ascent each of us had been on the Arrow four times before and twice we had set out together for at least three days' work. On Memorial Day, 1947, the route became the bed of a waterfall and ended in a precarious rappel. On Fourth of July weekend, much was learned during two days and a night on the rock, in which Second Error was attained for the first time. Better equipment was needed. We had thought ourselves in the pink of condition, but after only two days the state of nervous and physical exhaustion dictated retreat and far more rigorous preparation for the next attempt.

Several bivouacs on cliff walls, with or without warm clothes, taught us not to expect much rest on a climb. I took a hike the length of the John Muir Trail, practicing making long marches with little or no water. Doing that for four days in one's own home is good enough practice for mastering thirst — for learning, that is, how much thirst is to be safely endured. If one lacks time for long periods in the mountains, running steadily for an hour or so is a good way to build up the heart, lungs, nerves, and muscles for the long endurance at higher altitudes needed by any kind of mountaineering activity. To prevent the onset of cramps one needs brisk calisthenics to train climbing muscles far beyond their normal capacities. On the Arrow, failure to hold oneself to comparable preparations may be sufficient to scuttle a team's most carefully laid plans, and it has done so more than once.

For prospective Arrow climbers, it is important to have or acquire experience and competence with things mechanical; a manual acquaintance with forces, materials, and their relationships is a must.

This brings one to the matter of practical philosophy. One cannot climb at all unless he has sufficient urge to do so. Danger must be met — indeed, it must be used — to an extent beyond that incurred in normal life. That is one reason men climb; for only in response to challenge does a man become his best. Yet any do-or-die endeavors are to be condemned. Life is more precious than victory. In the safest possible climbing on the Arrow there is more than enough stimulus from probable and present danger. To know one's limitations and to keep within them is the essence of good sense. A comparatively weak party, sensitive to its weak points and keeping within their limits, will outlive and outclimb the strongest team, which proceeds indiscreetly.

One thing is not an adequate motive for climbing; that is egotism or pride. Yes, most of us who climb usually play to the crowd, as such an article as this may demonstrate. However, mere self-assertion alone has a low breaking point. To keep going day after day under heart-sickening strenuousness requires a bigger, more powerful faith than in oneself or in any concept of superiority.

Conversely, I feel that a man who, through emotional temperament or habit, is used to the false stimulus of alcohol has two strikes against him before he undertakes a long climb. The psychological impact of continually new and increasing difficulties while one's physical resources seem to be running down is enough without being fettered by an undisciplined imagination or by emotional crutches. Human limitations are indeed more serious than the natural ones to be faced.

A brief description of the first ascent may illustrate some of the foregoing points. In 1937 the 350 feet to First Error took 6 hours; 35 pitons were used for protection. In the 1947 ascent of the Arrow, we passed that point, hauling our 30-pound pack between us, in just 3 hours, using no more than a dozen pitons. Time was a major limiting factor and all possible haste was made when there was a chance. Nearly half the distance, 650 feet, was beat out the first day in the thirteen hours before darkness fell.

On the second day increasing problems really began slowing us down. We rope-traversed from the detour going out to Second Error back into the narrowest portion of the chimney where it slashes nearly 100 feet into the heart of the cliff. At midday we arrived at the vertical headwall of the chimney where Wilts and Austin had turned back on their second attempt after two and a half days. From then on the class-6 climbing began in earnest; 350 feet were made the second day, 200 each on the next two, and the last 50 feet on the morning of the fifth day. The first pitch of this sort, 150 feet long, was mostly rotten granite. Salathé led for eight hours without relief, save for the interruption of darkness. Two pitches above this point, massive, overhanging blocks had to be climbed by the exceedingly wide cracks between them. Often there seemed no evident route at all.

After the second day our muscles no longer cramped and we put thirst in its place. Bivouacking on the chockstones with our feet dangling, our backs aching where they were being nudged by granite knobs, and our shoulders tugging at their anchors, we got little sleep. Cold winds barely permitted us to keep warm enough for the rest essential to the digestion of food. The hours until dawn [that] should permit the greater comfort of climbing were passed largely in talk. Food, sleep, and water can be dispensed with to a degree not appreciated until one is in a position where little can be had.

Future Arrow climbers need not worry about varying the route; there is problem enough finding just one route, let alone fretting about alternatives. It should be noted in all fairness that on the first ascent the bolt-removing hammer was lost on the first day, necessitating the ruination of nearly all existing bolts. Extra hangers for the upper reaches were needed. Most of the holes are therefore hopelessly jammed with broken-off bolts. The work will have to be done all over again by the next party.

Getting off the climb requires a long rappel down the narrow confines of the chimney. However, we prusiked from the Third Error to the rim on a fixed rope, since friends were on hand to help rig it.

Frank Kittredge, then superintendent of Yosemite, asked if the 1947 Labor Day ascent of the Lost Arrow were not "the longest and most difficult high climb on record, presumably on sound rock . . ." It is merely pointed out that Lost Arrow granite can often be far from sound. The Lost Arrow can be climbed again, perhaps in only four days. At any rate, its superb challenge is there. To those who made the first vertical traverse of its Four Errors it stands as a symbol of high and unforgettable adventure.

ORDEAL BY PITON

Allen Steck

Excerpted from the *Sierra Club Bulletin*, May 1951

This story is not unique in the relatively short history of class-six climbing — there are many two- and three-day ascents listed today in the Swiss, Austrian and Italian Alps; indeed, directly across from Sentinel Rock, in the Yosemite Valley, is the unmistakable spire of the Lost Arrow, climbed from its base for the first time in September of 1947. This five-day ascent by John Salathé and Ax Nelson was considered the greatest achievement of its kind in the history of tension climbing.

The Sentinel climb was of equal rank, perhaps even surpassed it — who can say? John used to tell me, as we waited out the sleepless bivouacs, that he couldn't decide which was "better." "You know, Al," he'd say, looking out across the valley at the Lost Arrow, "it's still a pretty good climb. You and Long ought to climb it next." My answer was a despairing grumble: my next climb was going to be Sentinel Dome in a wheelchair.

I lay awake many a night in Berkeley wondering what this north wall was like above the buttress; it was almost an obsession with me. This sort of feeling is indeed strange to the hiker or fisherman, yet it is typical of the climber.

Many have questioned the quality of this sort of achievement, deploring the use of pitons, tension traverses and expansion bolts, but the record speaks for itself. This is a technical age and climbers will continue in the future to look for new routes. There is nothing more satisfying than being a pioneer.

The lure of the Sentinel Wall goes back to 1936, when Morgan Harris, William Horsfall and Olive Dyer made a reconnaissance on the north face. Rising a full 3,000 feet from the grassy floor of the Yosemite Valley, its sheer north exposure presented a fantastic problem in route finding; true, there was only one possible route (i.e., the Great Chimney), still there was the big question: How to use it? They reached the Tree Ledge, a prominent sandy terrace 1,500 feet above the floor, at the very foot of the north wall proper. Although no records exist, undoubtedly Charles Michael and William Kat, in their explorations of the cliffs, had ascended over easy class-four ledges to this terrace.

Several years later Morgan Harris and Dave Brower succeeded in reaching the Tree Ledge, and from the westernmost portion of this ledge they pioneered a route across the west face of Sentinel Rock and up its broken south side. The north wall remained untouched until the early forties, and, after several attempts by Robin Hansen,

Jack Arnold and Fritz Lippmann, a high point was finally established some 150 feet above the Tree Ledge, to the right of the huge buttress that lies up against the lower portion of the wall. The difficulty was severe, but each attempt added to the knowledge of the route. It seemed of little concern that there was over 1,300 feet of tougher climbing yet to do. That problem would take care of itself eventually.

In the fall of 1948, Jim Wilson and Phil Bettler took the initiative and reached a ledge 100 feet still higher, setting a new record. Then in October 1949 a four-man party — Phil Bettler, Jim Wilson, Bill Long, and I — arrived at the Tree Ledge prepared to make the first bivouac on the face, and was able to climb some 200 feet past the old high point. We passed the night on a loose, tilted chockstone directly beneath the 60-foot, 100-degree "Wilson Overhang." One person could stretch out comfortably, but unfortunately there were four of us. No one was able to sleep but Phil, who had taken one of Jim's backache pills to ease his headache — they were knockout pills, a decided must for any climber's bivouac equipment. Cursing Phil for his contented snoring, the rest of us waited out the night. Morning came and we continued up over the overhang, admirably led by Jim, to a new high point about 450 feet above the Tree Ledge. All eight leads were various degrees of class-six climbing, and over fifty pitons had been necessary. Then came the remarkable ascent over the 1950 Memorial Day weekend.

Bill Long and Phil Bettler, in a two-day ascent, succeeded in reaching the top of the great 800-foot buttress, and thus the first major problem of the wall was conquered. Above the top of the buttress stretched the final 700-foot face, whose broad expanse was broken only by the Great Chimney, a large dark cleft easily seen from the valley. This still remained the only possible way to the summit.

The first sixty feet (the Headwall Lead) above the buttress is smooth, vertical granite. The Great Chimney is over 100 feet to the left; it seems impossible to reach even by a tension traverse. Three hundred feet above, the Chimney narrows down to less than a foot and the walls are bare and overhanging. You may get into the Chimney, but 'The Narrows' looks doubtful. Thus had Long and Bettler reported the situation at the top of the buttress. The Narrows seemed — and ultimately proved — to be the most spectacular lead on the entire wall.

As on the Arrow, the route here was unmistakably clear; we joked about who was going to be the first to make the terrible 150-foot swinging traverse into the Chimney, but it seemed unlikely that this was the easiest way. There were a few small water cracks leading up the headwall that looked "feasible," to use the word loosely. In June, Jim and I made the first all-out attempt on the wall. As charter members of the recently established "Berkeley Tension Climbers' Running Club," we conditioned ourselves for the five-day attempt by covering the standard cross-country course in the Berkeley Hills. But it was of little avail; on the first day a falling rock severed our rappel rope on the second lead and we had to retreat. Leaving our supply of water — two gallons — and some fruit up on the wall, we rappelled as best we could to the Tree Ledge.

On June 30, while the rest of the RCS held its annual Minarets climbing trip, John Salathé and I climbed up to the Tree Ledge, prepared for another long siege. At the foot of the buttress we sorted our supply of hardware: fifteen carabiners, ten or so horizontal pitons, about eight angle pitons, and twelve expansion bolts plus hangers. We also carried a 300-foot rappel and a 120-foot quarter-inch hauling line for the packs, along with a little dried fruit. Our water, more dried foodstuffs, and a small can of tuna were up on the ledge 200 feet above, where Jim and I had left them.

Two days brought us over now familiar ledges to the small cairn on the buttress — 800 feet, fourteen leads (all class-six in part or in whole), and some eighty pitons later. From there on all was still unknown. We were to be another two and a half days reaching the summit, only 700 feet above, but requiring eleven leads and some seventy-six pitons plus nine bolts. The upper part of the chimney is broken, and many of the leads were composed of short class-four stretches between class-six overhangs. The last lead to the summit was a no-foot class-four "scramble."

On the entire four-and-a-half-day climb, thirteen leads were made by John and twelve by me. The ascent of this wall was probably the toughest one that either of us had ever made, or ever hoped to make again. Though John has 51 years to my 24, the climb seemed to have little effect on his endurance; only toward the end of the third day did he seem to show signs of wear, but then both of us were ready to acknowledge the pleasures of simple backcountry hiking. It was just too damned hot.

Each afternoon at two the sun came from behind the wall and turned the face into a veritable furnace; temperatures up to 105 degrees were recorded down in the valley and there wasn't a breath of wind. We could watch the swimmers down in the valley, languishing in the cool waters of the Merced — one would dive in now and then and we could easily see the white foamy splash as he hit the water. The thought of suddenly finding myself in a cool fragrant spring was so maddening that it was hard to keep my balance. If only those swimmers would stop splashing! And this was only the third day! John never said much about it, but I knew he was thirsty. Standing there in slings, with his hammer poised over the star drill, John would turn his head and say, "Al, if I only could have just a little orange juice!" Up on that wall, oh what such a simple thing as a glass of orange juice would have been worth!

Inside the Great Chimney, I happened upon a little crack, glistening in the shadows. I remember watching, my lips tight and drawn, while a little bead of water seeped out and smoothly slid down the rock. It was barely enough to moisten my lips and wet my mouth, yet it was a wonderful sensation. We were so short on water that we could eat little during those five days. John left his dates in the chimney; he was tired of carrying them. I threw my food away upon reaching the summit. All in all I would guess that we ate half a pound of food apiece — as a liberal guess!

With ten expansion bolts already placed, the second

ascent should do better, if there should ever be one. Six were needed on the Headwall lead. John stood in slings more than ten hours on that one. That day, the third, we made a total of only 240 feet. And after struggling over every foot of it, we were faced with the possibility of having to turn back. Not being able to go straight up, we climbed back into the chimney and eventually, through an inner chamber, reached a large ledge directly beneath The Narrows. Again the same old story — where to go? I can only say that there was little there with which to work. John finally made a bold attempt, using pitons upon which only he would ever rely (the double variety — back to back!); hanging almost horizontal, he was barely able to reach around to the outside of the chimney. The piton crack that he found made the lead. The Narrows were behind us!

The leads above here were agonizing in the hot sun. Still no wind. The packs got jammed in the chimneys, causing a great deal of wear on the nerves; there were bitter words, and we weren't afraid to let our tempers explode. When Ax Nelson heard of our plans, he remarked once to John, "If you expect to make the top, Al will have to be every bit as stubborn as you!" John agreed that I was.

The awful thirst. The overpowering heat cannot be described in simple words. Once on the top we could see the thin foamy line of the stream down in the gorge. We were on top, sure, but the ordeal wasn't over. We had yet to get down to the water that was staring us in the face. I slowed down for John as long as I could stand it, and then bolted down the couloir. I paid bitterly for my haste, for I descended into steep chimneys and had to claw my way back up through the hot, dusty deerbrush looking for another way. My judgment was numbed by the thought of water. I tripped over bushes, fell over unseen ledges, and finally collapsed fully clothed into a pool at the foot of a small waterfall. This was the climax of the climb, a supreme climax! And I can say, in retrospect, that it was well worth the effort. The reason, the incentive, the motive for all this? It is an intangible, provocative concept that I shall leave to the reader to explain. Some think they know why; others despair of ever knowing. I'm not too sure myself.

THE NORTHWEST FACE OF HALF DOME

Michael P. Sherrick

From the *Sierra Club Bulletin*, November 1958

The shoulder of Half Dome can be surmounted, between waist-high cables on a ladder way of wooden cleats, by any tourist free from vertigo and willing to essay a rock slope of moderate steepness. The northwest face is something else again. Bestor Robinson and Richard M. Leonard, who pioneered rope climbing on the Yosemite cliffs in 1931, dismissed the northwest face long ago as "so awful it might as well be forgotten." Millions of casual visitors, endowed with less precise knowledge, have looked upward from the valley floor and arrived at the same conclusion.

—From "They Risk Their Lives for Fun," by Hal Burton

In the eastern end of Yosemite Valley rises Half Dome, one of the scenic wonders of the United States. The summit of this huge granite monolith has been the goal of mountaineers, rock climbers, and hikers since 1850; the first ascent of the dome itself was done in 1875. The northwest side of Half Dome is a vertical face of smooth granite 2,000 feet high. On June 28, 1957, after five days of continuous climbing, Jerry Gallwas, Royal Robbins, and I made the first ascent of this wall.

As early as 1945 thoughts turned to this wall with the idea that a feasible route might be found. Climbers studied it with binoculars from the bottom and from the sides but it was discouraging, as anyone who has looked down from the top knows. In 1954 a Sierra Club party of Dick Long, Jim Wilson and George Mandatory climbed about 150 to 200 feet up from the base. In this same year other persons became interested in this climb; Jerry Gallwas, Warren Harding, and Don Wilson began some reconnoitering on their own. They discovered that the broken bottom half could be climbed, and that there was a massive flake system ascending the top half of the face. The two problems were: (1) connecting the broken bottom half of the face and the flake system, thus making necessary a 300-foot diagonal traverse across a blank section of the wall (Robbins Traverse), and (2) going from the top of the flake system to the top.

In 1955 Jerry Gallwas, Warren Harding, Don Wilson, and Royal Robbins made the first major attempt. In three days they pioneered a route up 450 feet of the cliff using six expansion bolts, including one for a belay anchor, and one for a rappel anchor. With more knowledge of the problems and better equipment, this foursome hoped to return in 1956, but these plans failed to materialize.

On Saturday, June 22, 1957, Jerry, Royal, and I met in Yosemite Valley with plans for a second major attempt. We had assembled the best equipment available. We used nylon flight suit coveralls as outer clothing for Yosemite's comparatively warm bivouacs; underneath, a warm sweater over our regular climbing clothing. Polyethylene containers held our thirteen quarts of water (a little less than one quart per man per day). Food was kept to a minimum — a few cans of tuna, raisins, nuts, lemon juice, chocolate, and some particularly desirable packages of dates. We carried 45 pitons, including 18 horizontals, 16 angles plus knife blades and wafers, and about 25 expansion bolts. We had more than 1,200 feet of nylon rope — two 120-foot 7/16-inch climbing, one 150-foot 7/16 climbing, two 300-foot 5/16 rappel, one 150-foot 5/16 hauling, and one 90-foot 5/16 hauling. Jerry Gallwas had forged about half of our horizontal pitons out of chromoly steel alloy. These tough pitons survived a beating on almost every lead; some must have been used 15 to 20 times each. Jerry also made most angle pitons, which would fit cracks up to 2 inches or wider; they too held up, despite being used perhaps a dozen times each.

Our gear was hauled up in a so-called torpedo bag which was girdled lengthways by 6 to 8 separate ropes for stability. The bag was covered with a duffle bag to minimize wear on the main parts. To prevent falling rocks as much as possible (usually thrown by someone from the top), Wayne Merry placed a sign halfway up the cables warning people against throwing stones because there were climbers below. We carried a first-aid kit and a flashlight. The latter was used to flash to the ground an elaborate system of prearranged signals at the time of the firefall. The time was chosen when people would be watching the firefall and we would attract less attention. Thus we make known our plans, progress, and condition.

That Saturday evening we made the final arrangements with the park rangers, to whom we are indebted for their helpfulness. We packed our equipment into rucksacks in preparation for the next morning's pack in to the base of the climb. Wayne Merry volunteered to help us carry part of our equipment to the spot where we left the trail, after which he would climb halfway up the cables to place the warning sign.

On Sunday, June 23, after an uneasy night in our sleeping bags, the four of us shouldered our packs at Happy Isles and hiked up the Vernal and Nevada Falls trail where we took the branch which leads to the back side of Half Dome. Just before we came to the rock massif itself, we parted company with Wayne and proceeded down to the right along the base of the towering cliffs carrying the extra load. Late in the afternoon, desiring to get a good start, Royal and Jerry climbed about 150 feet up the cliff and left a fixed rope. Only the first 30 to 40 feet were 4th- and 5th-class; from there on it was mostly 6th-class climbing. We ate our supper cold, having brought no stove, and we bivouacked at the base of the cliff — our last contact with the ground for five days.

Monday morning, June 24, we packed the gear which was unnecessary for climbing, into the torpedo bag and filled our canteens from a small streamlet issuing from the rock. When all was ready, one of us started to prusik up the 150-foot rope and when he reached the top the second man would start. When the first two would be at the top of a pitch, they would haul up the torpedo bag, which at the beginning of the climb weighed 55 to 60 pounds. If the bag became stuck part way up the pitch the third man would free it on his way up the pitch.

From the top of this rope we followed the complicated route pioneered by the first attempt in 1954. It was all difficult, strenuous, 6th-class climbing; when we came to the first blank, slightly overhanging stretch, the bolts were already in place. Above the overhang we reached a small ledge with an expansion bolt for an anchor. In 1954 Warren Harding had climbed 50 feet from this ledge and had left another bolt from which to rappel at their high point, about 450 feet from the ground. We managed to climb another pitch before dark and reached a small sloping ledge about 500 feet above the ground where we spent our first uncomfortable night tied to the rock. The ledge was large enough, but it sloped down at an angle of about 20 degrees; any movement caused a tendency to slide off.

On Tuesday morning, June 25, the climbing became somewhat easier. By one o'clock we had ascended 400 feet of mixed, moderate 5th- and 6th-class pitches, generally less steep in angle, and arrived at the base of the "Robbins Traverse" about 900 feet above the base of the rock. From all past reconnoitering, this part looked to be the crux of the climb. We had to traverse an exceptionally blank wall for a diagonal distance of about 300 feet, with a vertical rise of about 125 feet, to reach a prominent series of chimneys and flakes ascending the center section of the cliffs. Our problem was to cross this traverse with a minimum of time.

Royal started at about one o'clock and found the first pitch not too difficult. A zigzag series of cracks led diagonally to a small ledge about 80 to 90 feet away, from which a belay was made. From this ledge a small crack led up the blank wall for about 30 to 40 feet where it ended in smooth granite. After eight pitons, a series of seven expansion bolts was placed with arduous hammer and drill work by Royal and Jerry. These brought Royal, late in the afternoon, to a meager network of cracks which led nowhere. After placing three pitons he descended about 50 feet on the 150-foot climbing rope and proceeded to attempt a long and difficult, not to mention "airy," pendulum traverse in order to reach a series of cracks about 40 feet to the right. After four attempts he finally reached a hold and placed several pitons in time to return, leaving a fixed rope, just before dark. We spent our second night out on the ledges at the foot of the Robbins Traverse, our most comfortable bivouac because we had ample space to sit.

On the third day, June 26, we retraced the previous afternoon's climbing on fixed ropes and proceeded up the crack to a small ledge where we placed an expansion bolt for an anchor. One more long 6th-class lead brought us to the large ledge of the great chimney system which was so apparent from the side of the rock. From the ledge a fixed rope was left tied securely to the highest expansion bolts to facilitate a retreat back across the traverse if one proved necessary. Let this serve as a warning to future parties: it is not fixed on the top.

At ten o'clock we started up the beginning of a great

chimney and flake system which was about 1,000 feet above the base of the climb. Some of these flakes were huge in size and either leaned against the rock leaving a crack, or were separated from the wall forming a chimney. The first large chimney ended in an extremely difficult chockstone about 80 feet above the base. Instead of climbing the chimney we took a straightforward 6th-class crack about 3/4 to 1 inch wide which ran several feet to the left of the chimney. The flake was rejoined about 20 feet above the chockstone. From this point, strenuous 5th-class and some 6th-class stretches led to the top of the chimney system about 400 feet above us, 1,500 feet above the base of the climb. Of the pitches following the chockstone, one in particular deserves mention. Above the chockstone the chimney is filled with very large blocks of rock. One of them sticks out of the chimney about eight to 10 feet at a distance of six inches from the wall. Royal led up about 40 feet, placing four or five pitons. At the bottom of this block with a secure piton in place, he grasped up underneath the inside edge of the bottom of the block with his hands and "walked" out the vertical face of the cliff, working his way up around the lip of the block to a belay stance some 20 feet higher. Several pitches higher, with darkness rapidly approaching, we bivouacked behind the last large flake of the chimney system, about 1,500 feet above the base and 500 feet below the summit.

The fourth day, Thursday, June 27, was the worst day. By this time lack of sufficient water, food, and sleep, plus the enervating hot sun rays had fatigued us. With Jerry doing most of the leading, we climbed only 300 feet, but we had to bivouac 50 feet below our high point in a small indentation sloping downward behind a flake. Although straightforward, this 300 feet was composed of extremely strenuous and tedious 6th-class climbing. In the morning we had left behind the part of the flake system where the flake was out away from the wall, giving a chimney effect. The flakes were now a crack 1/16 to 2½ inches wide. As the cliff was absolutely vertical, the climbing of the flakes followed a peculiar pattern; they would zigzag from left to right and back again across the face giving the effect of climbing one overhang of about 30 degrees for about 20 to 40 feet with angle pitons driven straight up, then up a 60 degree sloping ledge with pitons driven down for about 20 to 40 feet, and so on. This tedious work took almost a whole day. Before dark Jerry led an additional 50 feet, leaving his pitons for the next morning. That night was extremely uncomfortable, but we were exhausted enough to doze a good part of the time.

On Friday morning, June 28, we packed into the torpedo bag all our gear that was not necessary for climbing or safety and threw it out about 30 feet. It fell the full 1,800 feet to the base of the cliff without touching the rock. Although we were only 300 feet from the top, some of the most difficult 6th-class climbing was still ahead. Jerry retraced his steps and climbed to the end of the flake system about 100 feet above. There, to our luck, was a 50-foot "Thank God" ledge leading off to our left, saving us from the prospect of a blank wall leading up to a tremendous 150-foot overhang. This ledge was traversed by walking and hand traversing to a series of 6th-class cracks, which led up to the left-hand side of the base of the overhang, ending in a small ledge barely enough for us to stand on.

From this point, the obvious thing to do was to traverse to the left out from under the overhang. This led to one of the most crucial pitches of the entire climb. With a bolt for a belay anchor, Royal led outward on several very poor 6th-class pitons, and then placed four expansion bolts which led to a small ledge where the angle lessened considerably. Jerry then made a curving traverse along a shallow crack which led to some easy blocks just under the summit. We landed on top at 6:30 p.m.

Warren Harding was on hand to greet us at the top, whence we all proceeded down the cables. Warren went down to the valley while the three of us returned to the base of the climb to recover our equipment. Since it was too late to return to the valley before dark, we spent our sixth night out in our bivouac suits. Saturday, June 29, we returned to the valley and checked in with the park rangers, fortunate to avoid publicity about an accomplishment which would only have been made into a sensation.

Some have said that we did the "impossible," and it is unfortunate that for decades the word impossible has been such a common term in the mountaineers' vocabulary, being applied to that part of a mountain which presents an extreme in difficulty usually too demanding for the equipment and technique of the day. But improvements in technique and equipment just keep on happening.

THE LONGEST CLIMB

Wayne Merry

From *Yosemite in the Fifties*, 1958

Barely a week after Robbins, Gallwas, and Sherrick completed their Half Dome climb, Harding, Powell, and Dolt began banging in the first of 1,000 pitons on the Nose of El Capitan. Some months later, Wayne Merry joined the party just as Powell and Dolt dropped out, and the rest is recorded here. Over the next half-dozen years in what was later coined the "Golden Age" of Yosemite climbing, the rivalry between Robbins and Harding in particular, and the clashing of their respective styles, would find historic expression as the Yosemite pioneers wrote chemtrails across the sky. For the first time in history, Yosemite Valley was the center of the rock-climbing universe. And what put Yosemite on the map, once and for all, was the first ascent of The Nose, truly the Father of all modern rock climbs.

—JL

Sixty years ago, Camp 4 in Yosemite Valley might not have been the grubbiest campground in all of

California, but it didn't have much competition. Neither did the handful of ragged climbers who frequented it on weekends. There weren't many of us, and we had the Valley of Light all to ourselves.

But if Camp 4, with its dust and shabby climbers, was squalid, the cliffs towering over it were sublime. Mornings, we'd awake to the lolloping of robins, and there would be the cliffs shining down on us through the pines. We'd lie there and wonder which new route to try today. We were rich beyond our wildest dreams, but we didn't know it.

We were not a little afraid of those big, unclimbed walls. It was a time of testing, of experimenting, of discovering limits. It was a golden time.

In the summer of 1957 I fell in with a particularly disreputable trio. We did a few climbs together and got on well, although I, a crew-cut seasonal ranger, was the "straight" man of the crowd. Warren Harding was the most arresting of the lot. He's a little guy, maybe five foot seven: a scrawny superstructure mounted on a set of tireless legs, a pair of shadowed, glittering eyes, a pile of black hair, an eldritch humor and an insatiable appetite for wine. He trained on red jug wine for every climb that I can remember.

Mark Powell's label was 'The Blond Giant,' and he was the raggedest giant imaginable — with excellent reason. He was one of the first to start pushing his limits free climbing, and he didn't spare his clothing, his equipment, or himself. The result was a spate of hard, new climbs and a tradition of bloodcurdling leader falls, which had somehow left him unharmed.

And then there was Dolt. Bill Feuerer was his name, but that summer he became 'Bill the Dolt,' or simply 'Dolt,' a name he was to make famous in the climbing world as the designer and manufacturer of jewel-like climbing hardware. He earned his nickname by performing a series of boggling blunders on the rock. Strong physically, he was a gentle and introspective person. His mild blue eyes and gentle mouth were framed by a Biblical beard, and an awed child was once heard to whisper as he passed, "Mommy, is that Jesus?"

These three were involved in a plan to climb the South Face of El Capitan, the awesome granite precipice that dominates Yosemite. It is so high, so unflawed, and so vertical that at that time only a few visionaries had even considered it possible. If its 3,000 feet could be scaled at all, it would amount to the most difficult aid climb ever done.

Many and wondrous were the gadgets conceived by Dolt to solve logistic and climbing problems and sketched on paper napkins at Degnan's Deli in the Old Village. Some were actually built: a winch to haul a lightweight cart up vertical distances; nesting aluminum channels to fit progressively wider cracks; even a modified basket stretcher for sleeping on a blank face. But eventually they could plan no more, and the assault began.

In the first seven days they pushed 1,200 feet of the most terrifying aid climbing done to that time, including several extreme pendulum swings to reach new crack systems. It was a landmark epic of "dangle and whack," and they retreated only when supplies ran out, leaving fixed ropes for new assaults. I was fascinated and envious, but confined to normal working hours. The attempt was stopped by the onset of winter.

The following summer I took a job mapping glaciers in Alaska, and lost track of the El Cap drama. All was not going well. Some sporadic attempts pushed the route still higher, but then Mark was betrayed by a worn shoe sole on a much lesser climb, and the resulting fall left him with a compound fracture and a permanently stiff ankle. The powerful Powell was out. So too was Dolt; for various reasons, he'd had enough. Harding was a leader without a team, and in early autumn of 1958 I got a call from him. Would I come? You bet I would! So would Rich Calderwood, a strong young cliffhanger from Fresno, and George Whitmore, a quiet, capable mountaineer who doubled as a pharmacist when he could be pried out of the mountains.

There ensued an Indian summer of weekend fiascos. We would leave classes and work on Friday night, drive for hours to Yosemite, and spend much of Saturday just climbing the fixed ropes to the previous high point. On Sunday we would gain a few feet, fix ropes, and cut and run to get back to town in time for work or school. It was a losing effort. So were Monday classes.

The rangers, too, were getting increasingly irritated. Valley residents knew when we were on the rock, and would park by the road to watch. Soon crowds formed, complete with traffic jams; before long, Smokey didn't like us much at all. Finally we were hauled before the

Chief Ranger, who delivered an ultimatum: finish the climb by Thanksgiving or get off the rock. Also, see that you fix ropes all the way so you can get off and not have to be rescued. And, finally, remove all the ropes and hardware when you leave.

So we went to work collecting ropes and food, made peace with employers, professors, and wives, and lit out for Yosemite on the last of October, for one last, all-out try. On the way, Harding pulled over at a liquor store in Merced to pick up a "summit kit" of champagne and proper glasses. We were acting pretty cocky, but there was a tingle like molten lead in our veins, and a do-or-die feeling in our guts. The bets seemed pretty even.

We strategized in Camp 4, over wine. George and Rich would relay supplies up the ropes while Warren and I pushed the route ahead. John Whitmer and Ellen Searby would aid on the ground at first, then take the trail to the top to meet us. Finally, there was nothing more to say.

And so we went — up the trail to where the wall leaped out of the ground like a castle; up the springing ropes, dangling packs tearing at our waists, into the sun and the white granite; up past the rusting pitons that secured the ropes, cotton-mouthed with apprehension. Questions nagged at us: had the ropes been chafing in the wind, or been nicked by falling rocks? Little darting shocks ran through us each time the ropes slipped over some unseen irregularity above. The upper half of the face leaned over us, incredibly high and forbidding. How far would a body fall free from up there before it touched the cliff, and how long would one have to savor the flight? We climbed far apart, one on each fixed rope.

We rested at Dolt Tower. Here was Dolt's infamous winch, with which we had earlier tried to haul supplies 1,200 feet to the Tower; here we now added cached supplies to our already-heavy loads. It took us another four brutal hours to reach the end of the fixed ropes and Camp 4, 600 feet above. Even though we had refined the climbing of fixed ropes with sliding prusik knots into perhaps its most efficient form, it was still a tedious, strenuous, painful business. Later parties, using the new mechanical ascenders (Jumars), would manage this stretch in a fraction of the time.

Camp 4 was big enough to sleep two, with feet pendent. To one side was a small, sloping shelf. Only Harding was petite enough for it, and that provided he lay with knees drawn up and a rope railing augmenting his coefficient of friction. George, amiable but independent, opted to return to a lower ledge for the night. Rich and I slept well; Warren didn't. He was troubled by a recurrent dream of falling, and awoke with a start once to find that he had indeed slipped off the ledge and was dangling by his safety rope.

Just above Camp 4 hung the Great Roof, a spectacular horizontal overhang that jutted out 30 feet into the cold air. A crack led up under that barrier, but more we could not see. For us it was the Edge of the Wild — the gateway to the unknown labyrinth of overhangs on the upper face. We flipped for the lead, and Warren won.

He attacked the long vertical crack below the Roof with a great jangling of hardware. It turned out to be more sensational than difficult, but there was only restrained optimism; the Roof itself might still be impassable. Harding reached it. There was a long silence, then a gleeful shout. There was a crack leading off to the right.

Warren moved gingerly, driving pitons straight up and dangling below, then half expecting the grating and the ping and the downward rush as a piton pulled out; but none did. He ended his lead on a ledge so small I could see part of his shoe soles as he stood on it. He fiddled around for a long time there. To queries about the route above he was noncommittal, hinting darkly that he was glad it wouldn't be his lead. As I shouted at the soles of his feet, I saw a drill slip from its pouch and fall: so steep was the face here that it fell past without touching, without a sound, and vanished below. We were about 2,000 feet up now, well into the final wall. Everything was either vertical or overhanging.

Harding descended to Camp 4. Though much of the day had been spent just getting organized and only one lead had been made, we were happy. The Great Roof had been a tremendous psychological barrier.

The night was cold, the ledge hard. In the morning, Rich departed down the slender, dangling ropes. I swayed upward, hauling extra coils that pendulumed under me as I traversed the line under the overhang. I could hardly believe the exposure as I watched Warren prusik up ground infinitely more terrifying than anything else I had ever experienced.

With Harding belaying from the tiny ledge, I went to work on an expanding flake 100 feet high (we later named it 'Pancake Flake,' owing to its flapjack thickness), each piton loosening the ones below it. I had no idea how to do it safely. Somehow, with Harding's ribald encouragement rasping up from underfoot, I cobbled together a tottering trellis of pins and slings. I crawled up onto a narrow ledge hours later, with very big eyes and the stink of fear about me. It was incredibly slow progress.

Warren removed the hardware with ease, pulling some pins out with his fingers, and went on past, stopping finally at a sort of hollow 80 feet higher. There the day ended. We dined, standing, on raisins and sardines. Then it was time for bed. I drove a line of pitons into the crack behind my foot-wide ledge and tied off a row of rope loops. Through these I threaded my Army surplus mummy bag, and into this cocoon insinuated myself after much struggle. There was no place to rest my head, so it hung limply at the end of my neck until I finally arranged a sort of sling for it with some cord and one dirty sock. Warren was even worse off. A medley of muttering, thrashing, and obscenity drifted down through the dark and kept me awake until midnight. About 3:00 a.m. I snapped awake as the piton supporting my feet and lower legs suddenly ripped out. The metal had contracted slightly in the cold. All the other pegs were loose, too. By the time dawn smeared the sky we were aching, groggy, irritable, and anxious to get moving.

There followed a most unpleasant day. The autumn sun beat with astonishing force into the south-facing dihedral. Warren, leading directly above, found the cracks completely choked with dirt and dry moss, which he had to remove with the pick of his hammer before pins could be placed. He was strangled by dust, and the larger clods beat at my head or pulverized as they fell. There was no evading the choking powder. Our eyes were gritty. We were gaggingly thirsty all day, and drank all but a taste of our remaining water.

Late that afternoon I became urgently uncomfortable: There had hardly been a convenient latrine for two days. Reaching a foothold, I asked Harding to hold me on tension and tended to the matter, half hanging in space. A plastic bag served well. In the relaxation of relief, I gazed benignly at the distant throng of El Cap watchers in the meadow, then slowly became aware that many of them were clustered around something that flashed like a great lens. To check, I smiled and waved. In the mob around the telescope, someone produced a white flag and waved back vigorously. On El Capitan, there is no room for modesty.

That evening we hauled up onto a series of excellent ledges, dubbed them Camp V with complete lack of imagination, and supped on dry pumpernickel, canned tuna, and a can of peaches. A scant cup of water remained. I hoarded my share in the peach can for early morning, then fumbled and dropped it off the edge.

That night demoralized me, and so did the morning vision of the Merced River, winding cool and green through the chasm below. It was my lead that morning. I placed two pins after vast temporizing, clinging to the wall like a limpet — and knew that it was not my day. Then, below, I heard a welcome voice. George had arrived with more rope, hardware, and water. I almost jumped back to Camp V. Between slobbering guzzles, I broached the question: "George, you wanna trade off with me for a day? Must be a drag, those fixed ropes. I'll go down to Camp 4 and bring up a load for you. Whaddaya say?" George agreed, but I don't think he was fooled.

I was right — it wasn't my day. On the rappel down, the single strand of nylon slipped to one side of the shoulder pad and burned into my shoulder. I couldn't stop to adjust it. The primitive over-the-shoulder friction rappel was too hard to hold. So I continued down, howling blasphemy. (Six decades later, the scar is still there.)

Above, the others were having their own species of pain. The climbing was hard, with smashed fingers, dropped pitons, and near-falls punctuating the pitches. But they discovered a fine big ledge — triangular and six feet on a side — that promised badly needed sleep without retreat. Soon after, I arrived from below to find George and Warren sitting on this fine ledge (Camp VI) in thirsty silence.

Then Rich arrived up the nylon highway, bringing fresh water supplies. The water and his obvious delight at our progress touched off a sort of reunion party. We laughed, recounted adventures, and horseplayed, milling around on the little ledge all clipped in, of course, to anchors. Or so we thought. Then Rich leaned back, and his anchor wasn't fastened. For an awful moment he teetered at the brink, until someone grabbed him.

Again it was time for Rich and George to leave us, slipping down the elastic threads into the void. What a job they were doing! They had all the work and none of the glory. The physical effort was enormous, and the work would have been dull except that they had to check and recheck every move, every item of equipment. They were working unbelayed, and the slightest error could mean a quarter-mile plunge.

The climbing was straightforward that day — uncompromisingly vertical, but the cracks were good. It was just as well. Strain, dehydration, and sleeplessness were taking their toll. Worst of all, a veil of cirrus spread out of the west to dim the sun. This was November, and anything could happen. Late that day, a thin drizzle whipped in on a west wind; scud wafted below us as we retreated to Camp VI. The temperature dropped, and the drizzle became sleet, then snow. Far below, on the exposed prominence of Dolt Tower, George stopped his upward haul and bivouacked. The first blast of wind destroyed his waterproof covering, leaving his down bag exposed to the elements.

Warren and I were luckier. We had an excellent tarp and could rig it firmly like a shed. Still, this weather had an ugly look to it. We had both seen similar storms plaster the cliff with ice, and a bad ice storm could wipe out our frail lifeline — or us. It wouldn't take even that; badly sliced ropes would be hideously dangerous to rappel.

The night passed without respite, and another day blew in, bearing snow. This was our tenth day on the rock. No one, as far as we knew, had ever spent so long on one cliff. We huddled under the slatting tarp, counted the remaining rations — three candy bars apiece. Should we try to retreat through the storm, or hope for a break? The hanging ropes, vanishing into a swirl of snowflakes, were not inviting. We decided to wait until tomorrow. If it looked like a break, we would go for the top and not stop climbing until we were there. It couldn't be that far now. Down below, George huddled in his wet bag, miserable and sleepless. He was determined to move up as soon as he dared.

At first light Warren stuck his head out. "It's clearing!" We gobbled a Baby Ruth, gathered our gear, and began the frightening climb up the wet ropes and the slick black wall toward the sunlight touching the rim. We climbed slowly as the rock dried, sometimes warmed by sunlight, sometimes chilled as a cloud swept gray around us. Warren struggled up a short free bit, nailed a slow bulge, and saw at last the final overhangs, two pitches above him. Then he heard a shout from above, and a rope snaked through the air toward us. The end dangled 10 feet clear of the rock.

John Whitmer's head peered down from the summit. "Hey, why don't you guys come on up the rope and have some hot food and a good rest, and go down again and finish it tomorrow?" He was deeply concerned, sure that we must be in bad shape. Warren's reply was unprintable. John vanished, rebuffed, but the rope remained. We ignored it.

Working up an almost-vertical trough, I found it barred by an enormous overhanging rock. I drove a piton up under it to move right, but the block shifted with a hollow crunch. My scalp prickled. One bolt remained;

I placed it to one side and moved around the block to a good foothold, anchored there, and brought Warren up. Through intermittent mist we surveyed the last pitch: 60 feet of clean cracks ending in a towering, three-tiered overhang with no cracks. And we were out of expansion bolts. Warren was wild with frustration, cursing bitterly at Rich and George. Where were they when they were needed? He would never climb with either again! As if in answer, a voice drifted up from below, and George's head appeared in the mist. He had brought some bolts.

In the dusk we ate our last candy bars. Warren donned a headlamp. I anchored into a standing belay, leaning gratefully against the slings. George settled stoically onto a sharp pinnacle. And darkness came.

That night remains blurred in my mind. I can remember the rustle of an icy breeze in my parka hood, the faint sound of a car horn far below, George twisting uncomfortably on his spike. My feet cramped on the little ledge and the slings cut deep. Often I nodded off and fell sideways, until my anchor came tight and jerked me awake. And always, always came the quick tap of Warren's hammer from above. Straight up, he was a tiny black spider in a flickering halo of mist, dangling under the overhangs with his body arched impossibly back, driving his hammer upward. He worked in grim silence, hardly resting, never complaining. Hours passed.

Toward morning the mist swept away; I could see Warren above me, hanging tiny and black against a skyful [sic] of frozen stars. Then he melted from sight over a bulge. His hammer tapped very slowly now. At long intervals, the rope inched upward through my hands. Behind us, the dawn grew.

For an eternity, the rope didn't move. Then it stirred and moved upward, gathering speed, slipping into the first rays of sunlight. A glad shout tumbled down over the rim of our world.

It was over.

Equipment:
- Carabiners: 50 steel and aluminum oval biners with lead team
- Many drills
- 125 bolts (The bolts were bloody awful. I wouldn't hang a picture from them today, but belayed from them then.)
- 2 European, wood-handled hammers
- Pitons:
    - Masonry nails
    - Original Salathé lost arrows
    - 3-inch oak wood wedges (rarely used)
    - 4 stove leg pitons
    - 3-inch aluminum "T" sections
    - Aluminum angles

Food:
- Kipper snacks (way too many)
- Canned fruit cocktail
- Canned tomatoes
- Jerky
- Canned tuna

- 2-gallon military surplus plastic bladder water container (tasted awful)
- Candy bars: O Henry, Baby Ruth, and Hershey's
- Trail mix
- Raisins
- Peanuts
- Canned cocktail wieners

Clothing:
- Heavy cotton plus-fours (like long knickers), military mountain pants
- Dacron T-shirt
- A wool shirt and sweater
- A thin Dacron batting-filled vest
- Nylon-cotton parka stocking cap
- Marine Corps combat boots (with modified Vibram soles), Kletterschuhe
- No rain gear (we got wet a few times)
- Down parka (the most sophisticated garment on the climb)

Miscellaneous facts:
- Number of people involved in the ascent: eight
- Amount of rope used on the climb: 4,000+ feet of yachting rope and manila
- How to lose weight fast with the El Cap diet: water rations: 1–2 quarts per day (Merry weighed 15 pounds less when he summited due to dehydration.)
- Hauling method: prusiking with 30–40 pound duffel bags attached to the waist

- Training method: Lots of $1.25/gallon red wine and pull-ups on doorframes
- Shelter: 8x10 rubberized nylon tarp for a lean-to on Camp 6.
- Portaledge: A Stokes Litter was hauled but never used

THE NORTH AMERICAN WALL

Royal Robbins

From the *American Alpine Journal,* 1965

I had been thinking about the *North America Wall* all year or even longer. We didn't want to use fixed ropes, but we also didn't know if we could climb the face. After climbing Proboscis the year before, in 1963, and before that the *Direct Northwest Face* of Half Dome and *Salathé,* I felt we'd reached the point in Yosemite where we expected to get up a wall. But we didn't expect to get up the North America Wall in particular. There were too many unknowns. For example, we didn't know where the route went or even if there was a route — El Capitan's southeast face lacked the continuous crack systems of the southwest face and the *Salathé*. Also, an El Cap route had never been established without some fixed lines. Well, we wanted an adventure, and climbing the southeast face of El Capitan without umbilical cords would be one sure way to have one.

The "we" consisted of Tom Frost, Chuck Pratt, and me.

Glen Denny wasn't available. We cast around, inviting Pat Ament from Colorado. He couldn't go, so we asked Yvon Chouinard. Yes, Yvon would be our fourth. It was good having him on the team. For one thing Yvon wasn't a Valley "regular," having done most of his early climbing in the Tetons. So we couldn't be accused of recruiting only Yosemite veterans. We knew, from Chouinard's past experience, that he was a very able climber, as well as an inventor and maker of pitons. But he had something else: He had a certain self-confidence. It was hard to quantify, but he had it. And if someone believes in himself, others believe in him too. We were no exception, and we were right. On the *North America Wall*, Yvon proved himself worthy again and again. Frost was Yvon's partner in business and the manufacture of climbing equipment, as well as his climbing partner on the first ascent of the *West Face* of Sentinel rock. I had climbed often with Tom, who was not only a very good climber, but also had a keen sense of humor. Our team was complete, and strong. We would need a strong team for this wall.

The Valley was still in the grip of an Indian summer. It was very hot, especially on south-facing El Capitan. Finally, on October 22, we could wait no longer — November and its storms would soon arrive. We carried loads to the base of the route in the sweltering heat. Yvon and Tom climbed the first pitch, and we four bivouacked at the foot of the wall. Yvon was nearly sleepless.

The next morning, with the relentless sun beating upon us, we continued. Tom and Yvon led, while Chuck and I followed with the bags. On the next two pitches, two pitons pulled out. The falls were stopped right away, but the pitons coming out showed the tenuous nature of the nailing.

The heat was withering. If it continued to stay hot, our 60 quarts of water would not be enough. We normally planned on a quart and a half per man per day. So under "normal" conditions (i.e. the north face of Sentinel Rock) we would have enough water for 10 days. But with the heat on a south-facing route we might run out.

We reached Mazatlan Ledge, 500 feet up, and spent the night. On the second day Chuck and I were to climb, with Frost and Chouinard "hauling," which meant prusiking with Jumars with a duffel bag attached to their waists. Pratt led past a cavernous overhang, and I led the next pitch up a line of bolts from an earlier attempt, to "Easy Street," a large, broken ledge at 700 feet. It's a good thing it was "easy," as we had entered the diorite, which, because of its dark shape on the southeast face, gives the *North America Wall* its name. Diorite by nature proved less reliable than the light-colored El Cap granite we were used to. "Easy" meant we didn't have to place many pitons in the diorite, which tended to break off in blocks. We climbed up the ledge a ways and bivied.

Slowed by our numbers and by the hauling, we didn't reach our previous high point of Big Sur Ledge until late on the fourth day. Tom led off Big Sur, traversing into unknown territory. He began by climbing diagonally left until he was 60 feet above us, then placed a bolt. We lowered Tom until he was about our level but 30 feet away. Then, since the wall was overhanging and he couldn't get purchase for his feet, we pulled Tom toward us with a hauling line attached to his waist — until we got him almost to the ledge — and released him. After several tries he got the range, and was able to swing to another ledge and place a piton. We lowered Tom again, and he performed another pendulum to a blank wall where he placed a bolt and returned to Big Sur, happy and fulfilled.

We bivied on the Big Sur Ledge, and on the fifth morning I led off using Tom's rope coming down from the bolt 60 feet above us. Chuck followed, and he and I completed the traverse across light-colored granite and climbed 200 feet up into the right-angling corner known as the "Black Dihedral," the feature that Tom had described as, "The ugliest thing I have ever contemplated climbing." Thus we got back into the diorite, with its treacherous rock. It was after dark by the time we returned to Big Sur.

The next day, the sixth, Tom and Yvon did the climbing up the Black Dihedral. It overhung so radically to the right that the belayer and the hauling team were safe from the rocks and debris loosed by the leader. Frost and Chouinard reached the top of the Black Dihedral after dark. When Chuck and I arrived we four set up hammocks suspended from pitons driven into cracks in the ceiling — "The Black Cave," we named it. With flashlights we could see centipedes crawling around on the roof above, but at least we couldn't see down. That would have to wait until morning. In the meantime Yvon, Pratt, and I had a good sleep in our nylon rip-stop hammocks, which Liz had created and sewn especially for this climb. Tom stuck to his tried-and-true hammock of elastic cords.

In the morning we could see we overhung the ground, 1,600 feet below us. It was an airy place, fierce with exposure. It was Pratt's and my turn to climb, so Chuck led off, pitoning from our hanging bivouac out to the edge of the Black Cave. We passed the camera to him so he could get that famous shot of us in our three hammocks. Then he returned the camera and followed a crack sideways. We could see the lower part of Chuck's body move horizontally from left to right. Then he disappeared by going straight up to a blank wall, where he placed two bolts and belayed in slings. I followed reluctantly. After all, it was my turn, and Tom and Yvon had done their part the previous day in getting us to the Black Cave.

When I reached Chuck, I complimented him on his lead. We looked around: The sky was darkening, clouds were building, and a south wind was blowing. It looked like rain, but if we could reach the Cyclops Eye — a large depression in the upper part of the wall — with its overhang far above, we thought we would be sheltered. We climbed as quickly as we could. Showers started before we reached the Eye late in the day. It was well after dark when Tom and Yvon, using our fixed ropes, joined us at our cave shelter.

In the morning we could see we overhung the ground, 1,600 feet below us.

That night we listened through a two-way radio to our friend Mort Hempel singing folk songs. Of course I was up on the wall and Liz down in the Valley. I didn't give her much thought at the time — on a climb, we didn't think about girls much, focusing instead on staying alive.

That's enough, for the moment. It's afterwards that we think of the women in our lives, and then they are serious business.

We learned from Mort that the storm we were sheltered from was supposed to last several days. That was not good news, but we were cozy for the moment and slept well.

The next morning, the eighth, it had stopped raining but the clouds persisted. I guess it didn't rain that day. I don't know. That was a problem for Frost and Chouinard. Chuck and I stayed where we were, protected by the overhang. Yvon went first, showing his mastery of climbing loose, rotten rock. Tom followed and led the second pitch of the day. Then, reaching the top of the Eye, Yvon placed pitons between overhanging blocks that weren't solid. It was again after dark by the time Tom and Yvon returned to our protected bivouac spot at the base of the Cyclops Eye.

The ninth morning was cloudy, and through the mist we saw that the Valley rim and the high peaks had donned a new coat of white. Snow covered the bald top of Half Dome. Chuck and I were wet and cold and would have liked to stay put, but it was time to get moving, so we ascended our friends' fixed ropes to the top of the Eye. Here, Chuck set up a belay in slings. From his stance I hand-traversed left and did some fancy nailing, slipping around on the wet, licheny rock and swimming in ice water pouring down from snowmelt. I did a lot of traversing on that pitch, getting farther and farther from Pratt, who was still belaying in slings. The exposure was terrifying. When you are climbing upward you get used to exposure, but when traversing the view below you is always new, so you don't get accustomed to the height.

Eventually, I climbed straight up, reaching a sort of cave near the top of the wall. We called our lucky find the "Igloo." It had a flat, sandy floor that could hold four people, and a big, flat boulder for a roof. We expected more rain, and the Igloo would be a good place to be if it stormed. Our friends hauling the loads soon joined us, and we spent the night there.

The morning of the tenth day was sunny, a fortunate turn of events for which we were thankful. Our bodies soaked up the sun's rays, and we luxuriated on the flat rock above the Igloo. It was less than 300 feet to the top. I got to climb that day, taking Tom's place as Yvon's partner. Tom said he wasn't feeling well, but I somehow doubted it. To this day, I think he was just being generous — letting me climb on "the summit team" — because the wall had been my idea. In any case I led off, starting with a big step to the right in the warm sunlight. I then traversed away from my friends on the flat rock until I reached a belay spot and brought Chouinard across. He went first to the final overhangs, which I led with difficulty to the top, thinking, "Well, this will give those who come after something to think about."

It was tough placing pitons. I got the bright idea of holding myself into the rock by hooking my waist loop directly to the piton from which I was suspended, thus facilitating a higher placement of the next piton. I thought this pretty clever, but Dennis Hennek, on the second ascent, didn't have any trouble here. (I was on top, watching.)

There was a bit of snow atop El Capitan and the white stuff covered the High Sierra, but the sky was blue and the sun was warm. We went down off El Cap by way of the East Ledges and reached the valley that evening, very satisfied. That's the way it is with good climbs — they leave you feeling satisfied.

THE SOUTH FACE OF MT. WATKINS

Chuck Pratt

From the *American Alpine Journal*, 1965

The historic first ascent of Yosemite Valley's El Capitan in 1958 opened a new era in Yosemite climbing. In subsequent years, three additional routes, each over 2500 feet in height, were established on the great monolith. El Capitan's great height, the sustained nature of the climbing and the resulting logistical problems required that the first ascent of these routes be accomplished in stages, with the use of fixed ropes to facilitate a retreat to the valley floor. Since the initial ascent of El Capitan, eight ascents of the various routes have been made, and climbers involved in this latter-day pioneering have gained great confidence and experience in sustained, multi-day climbing. By the summer of 1964, with new improvements in hauling methods and equipment, the time seemed ripe for someone to attempt a first ascent of such a climb in a single, continuous effort.

One of the few walls that had remained unclimbed

by the summer of 1964 and which afforded a challenge comparable to El Capitan was the south face of Mount Watkins. Rising 2,800 feet above Tenaya Creek at the east end of Yosemite, Mount Watkins rivals in grandeur even nearby Half Dome. Despite the obvious and significant challenge presented by the face, the mention of Watkins seemed to produce only a certain apathy in the resident climbers of Camp 4. Though many of them, including me, speculated on who would climb it, few of us were moved into action. Then one pleasant July evening at Warren Harding's High Sierra camp on the shore of Lake Tenaya, when the wine and good fellowship were flowing in greater quantity than usual, Warren showed me a flattering photograph of the south face and invited me to join him. In a moment of spontaneous rashness I heartily agreed, and we enthusiastically shook hands, confident that the fate of Mount Watkins had been sealed.

Several days later we were strolling through Camp 4, two rash climbers looking for a third, having agreed that on this climb a three-man party was a fair compromise between mobility and safety. However, our recruiting was unrewarded. The experienced were not interested; those interested lacked the necessary experience. By evening we had resigned ourselves to a two-man party when Yvon Chouinard walked out of the darkness. He had ten days to spare and wondered if there were any interesting climbs planned.

Within the week, after a reconnaissance trip to study the face and plan a route, we were assembling food, climbing equipment and bivouac gear for a four-day attempt on the face. The three-mile approach to Mount Watkins began at Mirror Lake. As we unloaded packs at the parking lot, two young ladies approached us to ask if we were some of THE Yosemite climbers. Yvon modestly pleaded guilty and pointed out our destination. They asked if it were true that Yosemite climbers chafe their hands on the granite to enable them to friction up vertical walls. We assured them that the preposterous myth was true. Then, with perfect timing, Harding yanked a bottle of wine and a six-pack out of the car, explaining that these were our rations for four days. We left the incredulous young ladies wondering about the sanity and good judgment of Yosemite climbers. And so the legends grow.

After following the Sierra Loop Trail for two miles, we eventually began contouring the slopes above Tenaya Creek until we reached the base of Mount Watkins, where we sought out a suitable camping spot for the night. In the darkness we noted with apprehension that the granite bulk of Mount Watkins completely obliterated the northern quadrant of the sky. The following morning we awoke grim and significantly silent. With lowered eyes we approached the base of the wall.

Unlike most major Yosemite climbs, Mount Watkins has very little climbing history. Warren had been 700 feet up some years before, and climbers had studied the face from the southern rim of the valley, but ours would be the first and only all-out push for the summit. On his brief reconnaissance, Warren had been stopped by an 80-foot head- wall above a large, tree-covered ledge. After studying the face three days before, we had elected to follow his route as it involved only third and fourth class climbing and would allow us to gain a great deal of altitude on the first day. By climbing a prominent corner at the left end of the tree-covered ledge, we could gain enough height to execute a series of pendulums in order to reach a comfortable-looking ledge at the top of the headwall, thus eliminating the necessity of bolting 80 feet. This ledge would then give us access to an 800-foot dihedral system on the right of the face. The dihedral eventually connected with a thin, curving arch leading westward across the face. We hoped this arch would take us to the great buttress in the center of the face and that the buttress would in turn take us the remaining 500 feet to the summit. However, these speculations would be resolved only after several days of sustained, technical climbing. The personal challenge, the unsuspected hardships, the uncertainty, in short, the unknown, which separates an adventure from the common-place, was the most appealing and stimulating aspect of the course of action to which we had committed ourselves.

Our immediate concern was transporting 100 pounds of food, water, and equipment up to Warren's previous high point. Loading everything into two large packs, Warren and I struggled up the handlines left by Yvon as he led ahead of us up an intricate series of ledges and ramps. By noon we reached the tree-covered ledge and the base of the headwall where Warren had turned back before. Having volunteerd to haul the first day, I began repacking our loads into three duffel bags while Warren and Yvon worked their way up the shallow corner at the left end of the ledge. Two free-climbing pitches brought them to a ledge where they investigated the problems of the long pendulums necessary to reach our goal for the first day — the comfortable-looking ledge 80 feet above me at the top of the headwall. By mid-afternoon Yvon had descended 75 feet, climbed across a delicate face and after trying for half an hour to place a piton, resigned himself to a bolt. Descending once more, Yvon began a series of spectacular swings trying to reach the ledge above the headwall. After numerous failures he finally succeeded by lunging for the ledge after a 60-foot swing across the face. Warren rappelled to Yvon and after dropping me a fixed rope joined him in an effort to reach the great dihedral which we hoped to follow for 400 feet.

Prusiking up the fixed rope, I could watch Yvon leading an overhanging jam-crack in the dihedral. From the ledge I began hauling all three bags together. I was using a hauling method developed by Royal Robbins for the El Capitan routes. It consisted of a hauling line which passed through a pulley at the hauler's anchor. By attaching a prusik knot or a mechanical prusik handle to the free end of the line it was possible for me to haul the loads by pushing down with my foot in a sling instead of hauling with my arms. The method was highly efficient and far less tiring than hauling hand-over-hand.

Yvon and Warren returned to the ledge after leaving 200 feet of fixed rope and we settled down for the first bivouac of the climb. After only one day on the wall it was evident to all of us that our greatest difficulty would be neither the climbing nor the logistics but the weather. It was the middle of July and temperatures in the valley were consistently in the high nineties. We had allowed ourselves one and one-half quarts of water per day per person — the standard quantity for a sustained Yosemite climb. Still, we were not prepared for the intense, enervating heat in which we had found ourselves sweltering for an entire day. Those mountaineers who scorn Yosemite and its lack of Alpine climbing would find an interesting education by spending a few days on a long Valley climb in mid-summer. Cold temperatures and icy winds are not the only adverse kinds of weather.

The following morning Warren and I ascended the fixed ropes and continued climbing the great dihedral, hoping to reach its top by the end of the day. The climbing was both strenuous and difficult as we resorted more and more to thin horizontal pitons and knife-blades driven into shallow, rotten cracks. However, our biggest problem continued to be the heat. We were relieved only occasionally from the unbearable temperatures by a slight breeze. Although we tried to refrain from drinking water during the day so as to have at least a full quart each to sip at night, we were all constantly digging into the climbing packs for water bottles. Every few minutes we found it necessary to moisten our throats since even a few breaths of the dry, hot air aggravated our relentless thirst. Even the hauling, which should have been a simple task, became a major problem. Yvon, who was hauling that day, exhausted himself on every pitch, becoming increasingly tired as the day wore on.

In the early afternoon, we were surprised by the

passing of a golden eagle across the face. Welcoming the chance for a brief respite, we ceased our labors and watched as the magnificent bird glided effortlessly high above us. Although he presented an inspiring sight, we hoped his nest would not lie on our route. In the days to come, this eagle would seem to make a ritual out of crossing the face, sometimes as often as three or four times a day, as though he were a silent guardian appointed to note the progress of the three intruders who labored so slowly through his realm of rock and sky.

By the end of the second day, we reached a group of ledges so large and comfortable that we named them the "Sheraton-Watkins." It was here that we were faced with the first major setback in our carefully planned route. The top of the dihedral was still some 200 feet above us. That 200 feet presented not only rotten, flaky rock and incipient cracks, but also the probability of having to place a large number of bolts. Now that we were within 200 feet of the prominent arch we had seen from the ground, we could see clearly that it did not connect with the large buttress in the center of the face, but that a gap of 100 feet or more separated them. The prospect of bolting across 100 feet of blank wall so appalled us that we began searching for other avenues of approach to the middle of the face. We were in a deep corner, the left wall of which presented messy but continuous cracks leading 80 feet to a ledge on the main wall. From this ledge, it appeared that a short lead would end on the first of a series of broken ramps sweeping westward across the face. It seemed the only reasonable alternative and we had just enough light left to ascend one pitch to the ledge 80 feet above before settling down on "Sheraton-Watkins."

We were up early the morning of the third day in order to accomplish as much as possible before the sun began its debilitating work. From our high point Yvon began the next lead. It was here that we began to literally walk out on a limb. We could see the broken ramps leading across the face for several hundred feet. Once we left the dihedral, retreat would become increasingly more difficult. Not only would the route beyond have to be possible, but we would have to consistently make the correct decision as to which route to follow. Using every rurp and knife-blade we had brought plus three bolts, Yvon succeeded in reaching the beginning of the first ramp. Then I began the first of three leads which were to carry us 300 feet across the face. Although the climbing was moderate fifth class, it required a great deal of effort. After nearly three days of climbing, the heat had reduced our strength and efficiency to the point where we moved at a snail's pace. Warren was barely able to manage the hauling bags without assistance and most of the afternoon was spent in getting our little expedition across the traverse. Although we had not gained much altitude, our efforts were finally rewarded when the traverse carried us into the buttress in the center of the face. Once again resorting to the indispensable rurps and knife-blades, I led a delicate and circuitous pitch past a dangerously loose flake to a curving arch. Following the arch as far as possible I descended, leaving what I thought would be a simple pendulum for tomorrow's climbing team. We were now situated on widely spread but comfortable ledges, and as we munched on our ever decreasing supply of cheese, salami and gorp, we caught a glimpse of our friend the eagle as he passed on his daily rounds.

At the end of this, the third day of climbing, we were well aware of our critical situation. We had brought enough water for four days. It was now obvious that we could not reach the summit in less than five. 700 feet remained between us and the giant ceiling at the lip of the summit and the route remained uncertain. We reluctantly agreed that it would be necessary to reduce our ration of water to provide enough for at least one additional day on the face. We did not yet consider the possibility of retreating although the prospect of facing the unbearable heat with less than an already inadequate supply of water filled us with dismay.

The fourth day proved to be one of the most difficult and uncertain any of us had ever spent on a climb. The sun continued its merciless torture as Yvon and Warren returned to the struggle. Warren found that I had underestimated the pendulum. After an agonizing effort, he finally succeeded in swinging to a ledge and I proceeded up to haul. By mid-afternoon, after climbing as slowly as turtles up the central buttress, we reached the most critical point on the climb. Above us a blank, 60- foot headwall topped by an overhang blocked further progress. Warren had nearly fainted several times from the heat, Yvon was speechless with fatigue and I was curled up in a semi-stupor trying to utilize a small patch of shade beneath an overhanging boulder. In an effort to provide more shade we stretched a bivouac hammock over our heads, but it provided little protection. For the first time we considered the possibility of retreating, but even that would require another day on the wall. It seemed that those very qualities which had made the climb so appealing might now prove to be our undoing.

Warren investigated the possibility of rappelling 100 feet in order to reach the opposite corner of the buttress. However, we did not want to lose 100 feet of hard-earned altitude, especially since we could not be certain that the left side of the buttress continued to the summit. After a barely audible consultation, we decided to try the headwall above us, hoping eventually that we would find cracks leading to the summit, still 500 feet above us. Warren volunteered to go up first. After placing three bolts, he came down, too exhausted to continue. I went up next and with extreme difficulty placed two more, the first direct-aid bolts I had ever placed, barely adequate, even for aid. Yvon took my place and after breaking two drills was able to place one more before relinquishing the lead to Warren. Instead of placing more bolts, the latter lassoed a small tree and prusiked 15 feet to a horizontal crack. With a magnificent display of spirit and determination, Warren continued the lead over the headwall, did some extremely difficult free- climbing and reached a ledge adequate for a belay. Refreshed in spirit if not in body, Yvon followed the lead in semi-darkness, marveling at Warren's endurance. Leaving a fixed rope, they returned and we all collapsed gratefully on barely adequate ledges.

By the fourth day Yvon had lost so much weight from dehydration that he could lower his climbing knickers without undoing a single button. For the first time in seven years I was able to remove a ring from my finger, and Harding, whose legendary resemblance to the classical conception of Satan, took on an even more gaunt and sinister appearance.

We slept late the fifth morning and awoke somewhat refreshed. Confident that we would reach the summit by nightfall, we ascended the fixed rope to study the remaining 400 feet. Once again we were faced with a critical decision. Continuous cracks led to within 100 feet of the summit, but it appeared that they would involve nailing a long, detached flake. Yvon led an awkward pitch that curved to the left around a corner. After joining him, I dropped down and swung to the left corner of the buttress. Still I was unable to see if that corner of the buttress continued to the summit. I decided to climb the cracks above Yvon. They were of jam-crack width and I pushed the free-climbing to my limit in order to conserve the few bongs we had brought. After a fierce struggle through bushes I was able to set up a belay in slings. That morning we had had two full quarts of water for the three of us. Yvon and I had already finished one quart and when he joined me I was surprised to find he still had a full quart. Warren had refused to take any water that day, preferring to give the climbing team every advantage. His sacrifice was a display of courage and discipline that I had rarely seen equaled.

With added incentive, Yvon led a mixed pitch up

a strenuous and rotten chimney, executing some gymnastics at its top to gain a narrow ledge. He joyfully announced that the next pitch appeared to be easy aid climbing and that the summit was only 200 feet above him. Anxious now for the top, I climbed as rapidly as I could while Warren struggled resolutely below with the bags. What we thought was a detached flake from below turned out to be a 100-foot column, split on either side by a perfect angle crack. The right-hand crack seemed to require fewer bongs so I quickly nailed my way to the column's top, a flat triangular ledge only 80 feet from the summit. It appeared that the next lead would just skirt the gigantic ceiling at the lip of the summit.

Yvon, resorting one last time to rurps and knifeblades, tapped his way to the crest of Mount Watkins just as the sun went down. His triumphant shout told me what we had all waited five days to hear. When Warren reached the ledge, he asked to clean the last pitch as he felt that he had not contributed enough that day! Warren Harding, who had been the original inspiration for the climb, whose determination had gotten us over the headwall below and who had sacrificed his ration of water after five days of intense thirst felt that he had not done enough! I passed him the rope and as he began cleaning the last pitch of the climb, I settled down on the ledge to my thoughts.

In the vanishing twilight, the valley of the Yosemite seemed to me more beautiful than I had ever seen it, more serene than I had ever known it before. For five days the south face of Mount Watkins had dominated each of our lives as only nature can dominate the lives of men. With the struggle over and our goal achieved I was conscious of an inner calm which I had experienced only on El Capitan. I thought of my incomparable friend Chouinard, and of our unique friendship, a friendship now shared with Warren, for we were united by a bond far stronger and more lasting than any we could find in the world below. I wondered what thoughts were passing through the minds of my companions during the final moments. My own thoughts rambled back through the entire history of Yosemite climbing — from that indomitable Scotsman Anderson, who first climbed Half Dome, to John Salathé, whose philosophy and climbing ethics have dominated Yosemite climbing for nearly twenty years, to Mark Powell, Salathé's successor, who showed us all that climbing can be a way of life and a basis for a philosophy. These men, like ourselves had come to the Valley of Light with a restless spirit and the desire to share an adventure with their comrades. We had come as strangers, full of apprehension and doubt. Having given all we had to the climb, we had been enriched by a physical and spiritual experience few men can know. Having accepted the hardships as a natural consequence of our endeavor, we were rewarded by a gift of victory and fulfillment for which we would be forever grateful. It was for this that each of us had come to Yosemite, and it was for this that we would return, season after season.

My reverie was interrupted by a shout from above and in the full, rich moonlight I prusiked to the top where Yvon was waiting for me. Warren had hiked to the summit cap to see if anyone had come to meet us. He returned alone and the three of us shared some of the happiest moments of our lives. As we turned away from the rim to hike to Snow Creek and some much-needed water, I caught a last glimpse of our eagle, below us for the first time. In the moonlight, he glided serenely across the face as majestic as always, and as undisturbed by our presence as he had been five days before.

TIS-SA-ACK

Royal Robbins

From *Ascent*, 1970

HENNEK: It was Robbins' idea, mainly. It was on a lot of guys' minds. Had been for a long time. I had thought of it, and when I loaned him my binos I figured he was taking a look. Meant more to him than anyone. He already had two routes on the face and couldn't bear to see anyone else get this one. He wanted to own Half Dome.

ROBBINS: In the afternoon Marshall-I call him Marshall because Roper started that, Roper likes to call people by their middle names, and such. Like he calls me "Roy," because he hates the pretentiousness of my first name. And I can't help that. Anyway, he likes to call Prall Marshall, so I will try it for a while. Marshall led a nice pitch up into this huge slanting dihedral of white rock streaked with black lichen: the Zebra. Those black streaks, legend tells us, were made by the tears of the Indian girl for whom I named the route.

PRATT: I belayed in slings at the top of this pitch which wasn't too bad, except at the start where you're 30 feet out with nothing in and then you start aiding with a couple of shitty pins. Royal liked the next pitch because it was loose and gave him an excuse to play around with those damn nuts and feel like they were really doing some good, which I doubt. But I am, it's true, rather conservative. Then we came down on fixed ropes and slept on a big ledge we called the Dormitory.

HENNEK: We would have been all right in the Zebra but we didn't have enough big pitons, even though we were carrying two sets of hardware. We needed about 10 two inch and a dozen inch-and-a-half pitons. The reason we had two sets of hardware is so one guy could be climbing all the time while another was cleaning. I led to the top of the Zebra and Pratt came up and started leading around the overhang at the top while Robbins cleaned the last pitch.

ROBBINS: From Hennek's hanging belay the crack widened to five inches. So Marshall used a four-inch piton, our biggest, endwise. It was weird, driven straight up like that. Then he got in a couple of good pins and used two nuts behind a terrible flake. Pitons would have torn it off. He didn't like it. Marshall hates nuts. He was talking about how it was shifting and then lodging again, just barely. I think he wanted it to come out so he could say, Robbins I told you so. But it held long enough for him to place a bolt, but it wasn't very good because he wanted to get off that nut before the nut got off the flake.

HENNEK: We couldn't see Chuck bolting above the overhang, but Glen Denny, who was taking pictures from across the way, got some good shots of us hanging there and Pratt working away. About dusk I lowered Royal out to jumar up and then I started cleaning the pitch.

ROBBINS: When I got up there, I saw Marshall had managed to bash three pins into unlikely cracks. There was nothing to stand on. When I pictured the three of us hanging from those pitons I Immediately got out the drill. Marshall isn't known as an anti-bolt fanatic-it's true about that thing on Shiprock, but that was mainly Roper—but there is no one slower on the bolt gun draw than Marshall Pratt. I got in a good solid bolt and we settled down for the night.

HENNEK: Royal says settled down, but he didn't get settled very fast. He was screwing around and cursing in the blackness, and then I heard this rip. He had put too much weight on one end of his hammock, and he ought to know better having designed the mothers, and then there was this explosion of screeching and shouting and terrible foul language that would have done credit even to Steve Roper. I thought it was funny. It went on and on. Fulminations in the darkness. I was amazed that he so completely lost control because he always seemed like such an iceberg.

ROBBINS: I had a unique experience the next day: placing 16 bolts in a row. It was just blank and there was no way around. But it was a route worth bolting for, and after a time I began to take an almost perverse joy in it, or at least in doing a good job. I put them in akk the way, so they're good solid reliable bolts, and I spaced them quite far apart, so I think that it's perhaps the most craftsman like ladder of that many bolts in the world. Still, I was happy to reach, with the aid of a skyhook, a crack descending from a ledge 50 feet higher. When Marshall came up he was raving. He raved a lot on that wall. He's an outstanding ravist, often shouting at the top of his lungs like Othello in heat. "Why, why, why," he shrieked, "Why didn't I re-up?" "Christ, I could be a sergeant by now, with security and self-respect. Why did I start climbing in the first place? Shit, I could have been a physicist, with a big desk and a secretary. A secretary!" he repeated, brightening, a leer breaking across his face. "But, no, no, I couldn't do that. I had to drop out of college. Because I . . . I," his voice rising in a crescendo. I, like Christian Bonington, chose to climb." I was convulsed. We were having a good time. Nobody uptight. No ego trips. But we were low on bolts and low on water. We would have to go down the next day. It was late afternoon and . . .

HENNEK: I'll take over here to save all of us from another of Royal's glowing descriptions of how the sun goes down. After a night on the ledge-and a rather long October night at that-we rappelled, placing bolts and dropping from one hanging stance to another. We all wanted to return. It was going to be a good route, and we left a lot of hardware at the base, to save carrying it up next time.

PRATT: But when next time came, in June, the summit snowfield was still draining down the face. It had been a heavy winter. So we put it off until the fall, and I went to the Tetons, Robbins went to Alaska to stoke his alpine hang-up, and Dennis went fun-climbing in Tuolumne Meadows and re-damaged an old injury so he was out of the running for the year. In October I got a card from Robbins saying he'd be up in a few days for the Dome, and when he didn't arrive it really pissed me off, and when days later he still didn't arrive I said fuck it and made plans to go on El Cap with Tom Bauman. Christ, when Robbins didn't show, people were looking for him on Half Dome, solo. And then when he finally came up several days late his mood really turned me off. He was tense and cold. He said he couldn't wait until Tom and I had done our climb; he was taking the Dome too seriously, so I decided not to go.

ROBBINS: When Chuck said he wouldn't go I was almost relieved. At least now he couldn't make me feel like I was dirtying the pants of American Mountaineering. I feel guilty with a camera when Pratt is on the rope. It's like asking a Navajo to pose, and I would never do that. Marshall hates cameras as much as he hates my puns and 5.10 psychos. He doesn't want anything to get between him and the climbing experience. He suggested I ask Don Peterson. Peterson had been up the Dihedral Wall and was hot to go on anything as long as it was difficult. Although he had never studied the wall, il didn't take much persuading.

PETERSON: We agreed to go up in the morning. Robbins was like a man possessed. He was totally zeroed in on Half Dome. He had a lecture date soon, and he had to squeeze it in. It rained like hell that night and looked bad in the morning but Robbins figured we might as well go up because it might not storm. I didn't like it but I didn't say anything, and we started walking up expecting to get bombed on any minute.

ROBBINS: Our loads were murderous. We stopped where the great slabs begin and gazed upward. Didn't know what you were getting into, did you? l asked, facetiously. "Well," replied Don, "it can't be any harder than things I've already done." I turned absolutely frigid. The tone of the next eight days was set right there.

PETERSON: What I didn't like was his assumption of superiority. Like he figured just because he was Royal Robbins he was the leader. Christ, I had done climbs in the Valley as hard as he'd done, and I did the Dihedral faster. Yet when we got up to the base of the wall he sent me to fetch water. I just don't buy that crap.

ROBBINS: On the way up Don asked if there was anything on the North America Wall harder than the third pitch. 1 told him no-as hard but not really harder. Well, then, he said, we shouldn't have any trouble with the rest of it. Mead Hargis and I have been up the third pitch, and it wasn't too bad. Oh, really, I said. Well, it might be a little easier now because Hennek and Lauria had to place a bolt. Oh, no, he said, we chopped it. We went right on by.

In a few hours we were at the Dormitory. It was strange climbing with Don. Like many young climbers he was intensely impatient. He was used to great speed and just going. Speed is where it's at. It's not the noblest thing in climbing, but it moves many. Still, I didn't expect to feel the pressure of Don's impatience running up the rope like a continually goading electric current. And I didn't expect a generation gap, but there it was. For eight days we would be locked in sullen conflict, each too arrogant to understand the other's weaknesses.

PETERSON: On the second day we reached the top of the Zebra. Royal belayed in slings while I led the pitch over the top. Right away there was this wide crack. Robbins told me Pratt had knocked a four-incher endwise into the five-inch crack. I screwed around for a while, wondering why he hadn't brought a bigger bong this time. I couldn't get it to work so I took three bongs and put them one inside the other and that filled the crack okay, but God was it spooky. Still, I thought it was a pretty clever piece of engineering.

ROBBINS: After Don made this strange bong maneuver, he reached the flake where Marshall had had his wild time with those tiny wired nuts. "It's been a long time since I've used nuts," said Don, to cut the power of any criticism I might have of his chocking ability. After he had put his weight on the second one, it pulled and he ripped out the other, falling 15 feet. He didn't like that, and this time he nested two pins first. But he still couldn't drive a pin higher as the flake was too loose so he put the nut back in and got on it. It was holding so he started to take in rope and as he was reaching for Pratt's bolt the chock came out and down he came, pulling the pins and falling 20 feet this time. I feared he might be daunted but he swarmed right back up the rope and got the top nut in and got on it and pulled in a lot of rope and got the bolt this time. Fighting spirit, I thought. I reflected how Don was a football player and how he must charge the line the way he charges up those pitches.

PETERSON: Robbins was rather proud of his bolt ladder and bragged about it while he was leading it. I passed his belay in slings and led on up to the previous high point, which Robbins called Twilight Ledge. In the morning he took a long time leading around several lips of rock. I was getting pretty antsy by the time he finished. Christ, was it all going to be like this?

ROBBINS: Above us rose a deceptive five-inch crack. Don went up to look at it and said do you want to try it? It won't hurt to try, I replied, but when I got up there I wouldn't do it without a bolt, and we had no bolts to spare. So for about an hour I played with bongs driven lengthwise, and with four-inch bongs enlarged by one-inch angles driven across their spines. It was distasteful as hell, and if anything came out I'd be right in Don's lap. I was trembling with more than exertion when I finally clawed my way to Sunset Ledge. When Don came up I was gratified to hear him say he didn't think he could have done it. Maybe now the tension would be eased between us. He probably wanted me to say, "Sure you could." But I couldn't give up the one point I had won.

PETERSON: It was a good ledge. We were halfway or more. It was my lead but Royal had a lot more bolting experience so he led off, placing a bolt ladder diagonally across a blank section. In the morning, I finished the ladder, nailed a big loose flake, and put in a bolt and belayed in slings. When Robbins came up, three or four pins just fell out.

ROBBINS: The first thing I did was put in another bolt, for above Don's belay rose another of those vile Five inch cracks, too big for our pins and too small to get inside. I launched an all-out effort, struggling and thrashing desperately in the slightly overhanging crack. Four months later I still bear the scars. The top of the flake was like a big stone fence without mortar, but l got across that and placed a few bolts and then nailed a thin horizontal flake. I placed seven pins there, and four fell out before I had finished. With two good bolts for a belay and hanging bivouac I was safe and happy with nothing on my mind but the next 800 feet. Don wanted to try the jam crack because I had said it was probably the hardest free climbing I had done on a big wall, but I told him we don't have time, man, which we didn't. I was very relieved, for I was afraid he would come up easily and go down and tell the fellows I said it was hard but he didn't find it so. What the hell, that would happen in the next ascent anyway. Let the pitch have a reputation for a year.

PETERSON: At about this point I wasn't feeling too happy. Robbins had taken almost a whole day to lead one pitch. I just didn't see how we could make it at this rate. I knew he had to place a lot of bolts, but it about drove me out of my skin wailing for him to finish. I felt I could have gone faster. We were using too many bolts when we still had this big blank section above us. What if we didn't have enough? But the only thing Robbins had to say was, "We can always turn back, or else they can pull us off." I didn't think we were going to make it. I had never gone so slowly on a climb in my life.

ROBBINS: I hated drilling those bolts. We had these extra-long drills that were all we could get at the last minute, and we had a long drill holder, too, so I was bending over backwards drilling, and drilling is plenty bad enough without that. Here I was working away and always this mumbling and bitching from below, and finally the shocking ejaculation, "This is a load of shit." From then on I felt I was battling two opponents, the wall and Peterson. I had learned to expect a grumble whenever I made the slightest error, such as not sending up the right pin ("Goddamn it! Everything but what I need!"), or forgetting the hauling line. I began to feel incompetent.

It wasn't really so much what Don said, it was that he said it. It was a new experience climbing with someone who gave his emotions such complete freedom of expression. I was shocked and mildly terrified by Peterson's dark passions bubbling repeatedly to the surface. It probably would have been healthier to have responded in kind, to have shouted, "Fuck you, Peterson," every time I felt scorn, real or imagined, coming my way. I didn't lack such feelings. The things I was calling Don were far worse than anything he said, direct or implied. But when I said them I kept my mouth shut.

PETERSON: On the fifth morning I had to use up three more bolts because there was another five-inch overhanging crack. I finally got into it and went free for 100 feet completely inside a huge flake. Then we had three straightforward pitches before some bolting brought us to a great ledge, where a ramp led up to a huge blank area below the summit. That night our water froze. In the morning I led up the ramp to a tight little alcove. The blank wall started about 30 feet up. It looked awfully big.

ROBBINS: As I nailed up to the blank area, I thought hard about our remaining 30 bolts. We would place some so they were barely adequate, allowing us to pull and reuse them. We had now traversed too much to descend. Those long drills were murder. I had three Rawl drills and another holder, and I used them to start the holes. They were extremely brittle, but I soon learned that a broken Rawl worked fine, and if they didn't break well,

I would re-break them with the hammer. I was saving three short Star drills for the end. I didn't get far that day. It was slow going. I used one drill seven times before discarding it. Don spent the night scrunched in his cave while I bivouacked in a hammock. The weather, which had been threatening, was holding well. The next day was an ordeal. Sometimes it took nearly an hour for one bolt. Whenever I wasn't drilling I had my head against the rock in despair and self-pity. And always that electricity along the rope, that distracting awareness that Peterson must be going mad. Poor Peterson, but poor me, too. Besides the hard work, there's something mentally oppressive about being in the middle of a large, totally blank piece of rock. I was sorry I had disdained bat-hooks, believing as I had that if you're going to drill a hole you ought to fill it with a good bolt. I was so far gone now that anything went. I just wanted to get up. But there was nothing to do but what we were doing. When Don came up to my hanging belay, the first thing he said was, "I was sitting down there for 24 hours!" That's energetic youth. Don had suffered as much sitting as I had drilling. That afternoon Don placed a few bolts, more quickly than I had, but with no more enthusiasm. The next day I again took over the bolting, inexorably working toward the barely visible lower corner of the dihedral leading to the summit overhangs. That edge of rock was our lodestone, drawing us like a magnet.

PETERSON: Robbins had hoped to do the wall in six days, but this was the eighth. We really wanted to get off and thought maybe we could. The bolting was going a little faster now with Robbins using the short drills and not putting the bolts in very far. He would place one well and then two poor ones and then another good one and then come down and take out the two bad ones and replace them above. He did this about 20 times. Robbins rarely said anything while he was working on a pitch. He was like a beaver working away on a dam, slow and methodical. At times I felt I was going to burst, just sitting in one place doing nothing. I like to climb. This wasn't climbing, it was slogging. But I had to admire Robbins' self-control. He had about as much unmanageable emotion as an IBM machine.

ROBBINS: We reached our lodestone just as the sun was reaching us. Don eagerly grabbed the lead, nailing up from the last bolt. Thin nailing it was, too. By stretching a long way from a RURP, he drove a knifeblade straight up behind the rottenest flake imaginable. II seemed impossible it could have held. I had vowed that I wasn't going to give Peterson an inch, but I weakened. I told him it was a damn good lead. It would have been too flagrant not to have done so. We were now on a ledge beneath the final overhangs. Above, gently pivoting with grotesque finality in the afternoon breeze, dangled a gangly form, mostly arms and legs, with a prophet's head of rusty beard and flowing locks. It was the artist, Glen Denny. He and the rock around him had already taken on a golden hue as I started up in an all-out effort to reach the top before dark. It didn't look far, but using two RURPs just to get started was a bad omen. I went as fast as possible, but not fast enough to escape Peterson's urging to greater speed. The summit tiers overlapped one another, building higher and higher like the ninth wave. On several, reaching the crack separating the folds was barely possible. On one, a hook on the wire of a nut saved a bolt. Everything happened at once as I neared the top. The cracks became bad, the light went, pulling the rope was like a tug-of-war, and I was running out of pins. I had just gotten in a piton and clipped in when the one I was on popped. As I got onto the next one the piton below dropped out, and then I was off the aid and onto a sloping smooth slab in the blackness, realizing I was really asking for it and picturing the fall and the pulled pins and hanging in space above Don. I backed down and got into my slings and cleaned the top pin with a pull, then began nailing sideways. Glen Denny is watching silently as I start to crack but I realize I am getting melodramatic and find myself looking at it through Glen's eyes, completely objectively and so cool down and feel with fingers the cracks in the darkness and bash away with the hammer smashing my fingers and pins coming out and me complaining in the darkness putting fear into the heart of my companion and asking him to send up his anchors so I can use them but he refusing and me saying to Glen that's the way it's been all the way up.

TEAM MACHINE (1976)

Billy Westbay

From *The Valley Climbers*

An alarm sounds at 2:00 a.m. Three bodies arise quickly and move, not with the usual dragging motions of an early rise, but with precise movements and an economy of action. They dress in costumes for the occasion a la Jimi Hendrix. All sit to a breakfast of king-sized omelettes, followed by beans, to get the day moving. Quickly, their gear is checked and found to be in order. They drive to the base of the Nose, and go through the final ritual of putting on E.B.s, swamis, and tape.

It's 4:00 a.m. We take off on the initial pitches, rehearsed a few days before, but this time under the light of headlamps. Darkness still engulfs us as we hit Sickle Ledge, although the false dawn begins to lend a hint of light. John assumes the lead and tackles his section of the route. Our plan is to have each of us lead approximately the third of the climb best suited to our own abilities.

John, the most powerful climber to come to the Valley since Jim Madsen, has the crucial task of setting the pace to Boot Flake, 40 percent up the wall, where I'll take over and lead to Camp 5, with the anchor leg going to Bridwell. Sacrificing the usual amenities of climbing in the name of speed, we tie figure-eights and clip them into locking biners for a quick rope-end exchange. As soon as John finishes a lead, Jim and I hit the jumars, racing to the next belay. In no time we are in the Stovelegs, where John, puffing under a full head of steam, blasts pitches off before we can smoke a cigarette.

Cramping hands quickly begin to affect us. We make a brief stop to pry them from the jumars and massage them open, then it's back to the vertical sprint; we can't afford to waste precious time. On Dolt Tower, we arouse another party from their dreams. Checking the clock, it's only a little past six. We're cookin'! The total commitment by each of us seems to bring the energy level to an unbelievable pitch. From a corner of my mind, I perceive this energy flow to be seen and felt equally by the others.

Standing on the toe of Boot Flake, I wait for John to finish hauling my pack and put me on belay. Time seems almost suspended for us this day. Our rhythmical upward motions are the ticks on our clock. When the call comes, I lean back, kicking in to the King Swing. Pitches fly by, as we reach Camp 4 by 11:00 a.m. It feels like nothing will stop us. Sweaters and non-essential items that might make a bivouac possible are jettisoned. Watching the gear float through the air, an uneasiness moves me. A check for thin spots on our three nine-millimeter ropes shows them to be okay, yet this doesn't block out completely my memory of the guy who, last year, set the record for the fastest descent from the summit overhangs when his rope was severed by a bolt. But the sweaters disappear, along with its mesmerizing effect, and I get back to pushing my leg to Camp 5, which we reach at 1:15 p.m.

The furious pace we've set begins to have a withering effect. Continuously vertical to overhanging pitches are draining Jim and John on the jumars, tied in with swami belts to save weight. We're slowing down, and it's a struggle to gain a second wind. After 2,200 ft. of jumaring, the Bird (Bridwell) finally takes the lead.

He had been on a dawn-to-dusk rescue the day before. With plough-horse persistence, he begins hammering away to Camp 6, getting there at 3:30 p.m. Hoping to find many fixed pins in the upper third, Jim is disappointed to find few. It means a lot more work, and energy is scarce.

The final pitches find us running short of 5/8" angles, 3/4" angles, and patience. All of us are overtired and edgy, which seems to create mistakes and problems. At one point the free rope hooks behind a large flake, and a rappel looks like the only way to free it. Working up a real frenzy, I manage to get it loose with much mad jerking, yanking, and cursing. Another screaming curse from Jim soon follows. Looking up in time to see a mass of slings flying toward us, I instinctively reach out and grab Jim's ladder before it plummets into the abyss. Tempers flare, and communications are reduced to shouts and anger. These erupting emotions reflect our frustrations and anxiety to finish. Somehow, energy and luck sustain us on the final pitches. El Cap in a day!

7:00 p.m. Three weary bodies stand on the summit of

El Cap. Beginning an epic descent in E.B.s, they return to the Valley floor seventeen hours after leaving it. Dumping their gear, the three pass slowly beneath the trees of street-lit Yosemite. Still wired, they ramble on, oblivious to the surroundings, and adjourn to the bar to share the hospitality of friends.

Billy Westbay died of liver cancer in 2000.

THE LAST PITCH (1976)

John Long

From *The Valley Climbers*

"Watch me close," I said to Ron, remembering my first time on this pitch, several years before. "This might get funky."

I felt anxious, amazed, primed — everything all at once. El Capitan in a day was a done thing. In this, the Indian Summer of traditional-style rock climbing, free-climbing a genuine big wall remained the last and greatest prize. We wanted to be first and here was our chance to close the deal, eleven pitches up the overhanging East Face of Washington Column.

From the start, I'd warned the boys that this last pitch might shut us down, so we were bursting at the seams from the suspense of battling all the way up here and still not knowing.

"Get us off this thing," said Ron.

Ron Kauk was only a kid. Seventeen, I think. I outweighed him by sixty pounds, but Ron had caught me falling many times, so I didn't question his hip belay. John Bachar, third on the rope, reached an arm from a patch of shade, passed me a couple slings, and said, "You're the man."

That helped. All the way up, we'd cheered and prodded one another as aid pitch after aid pitch fell to our free-climbing efforts, pitches that soon became classics: *The Boulder Problem Pitch*, with its fingertip liebacking and scrabbling feet; the *Enduro Corner*, a soaring dihedral that goes from thin hands to big fingers, right to the belay bolts; the thrutching *Harding Slot*, a claustrophobic, bottomless flare that was destined to dash the hopes of so many Europeans; and the flawless *Changing Corners*, a vertical shrine of shifting rock planes with an ocean of air below. For over a thousand feet now, the blond-orange cracks kept connecting in remarkable ways, and we kept busting out every technique we knew. Never before had we experienced a route so continuously difficult. To our knowledge, no climbers ever had.

Fifty feet to go.

My toes curled painfully inside my EBs, but I reached down and cranked the laces anyhow. Sweat dripped off my face onto the rock. We passed around the last of our water as I racked a few small pitons and several Stoppers and Hexcentrics on the sling around my shoulder. I slowly chalked up, glanced over at John, and said, "I'll take some tunes, if you please."

John reached into his day pack and punched the

button on our little cassette deck. Jimi Hendrix's "Astro Man," our theme song for the route, blared through the top flap. John flashed that insolent grin and said, "Rock and roll, hombre."

John Bachar. He looked more like a math geek than an athlete, with his elfin build, stringy blond mop, and two shiny silver buckteeth. Back in high school, I'd get midnight calls from John about his new climbs or boulder problems, meaning I immediately had to beg a car or even hitchhike to Stoney Point or Mount Rubidoux so I could bag these routes as well.

Meanwhile, John began his lonely quest to become the world's greatest solo rock climber, a ritual he practiced for an astonishing thirty-five more years before it finally took him out. But just then, smirking on that ledge, he was eighteen years old, and looked about twelve.

I took a last sip of water and shuffled out on the tapering ledge, around a corner and over to moderate lie-backing up the left side of the short pillar, ending at a 25-foot headwall.

All the way up, the rock remained diamond-hard, but here it turned to sand. Two summers before, on my first big wall, flambéed by a heat wave, I'd nailed this last bit via rickety pins bashed into a rotten seam. I'd wondered out loud, to Ron and John, how we might free-climb the section; one glance confirmed we never would. However, just right of the seam and straight up off the pillar, the vertical face bristled with sandy dimples and thin, scabby sidepulls. I'd have to toe off pure grain and yank straight out on these scabs, praying they didn't bust off. The only protection was several tied-off baby angles slugged into that seam.

While organizing our gear, I'd talked big about not bringing a bolt kit and about high adventure, cha cha cha. What an ass. I couldn't hang my hat on those pins. The only nut was in the lieback crack, ten feet below. It was one of those surreal fixes where I was plainly screwed yet somehow had to make do.

I reached up and grabbed the first sidepull. It felt serious just to hoist my feet off the pinnacle, and I stood sulking for several minutes. Here was the chance of a lifetime and I was too gripped to commit. Maybe Ron should have a go? He would race up this, I thought. Ron was the most gifted climber we had ever seen. He'd hiked the *Endurance Corner* like a staircase. Same with the *Harding Slot*. Nothing could stop him.

Ron first turned up in Yosemite when he was fourteen and it was like releasing a shark into the ocean. The elements were living things in him, and the rock and even the Valley itself seemed fashioned just for Ron. In some nameless way, fundamental as chain lightning, Ron Kauk was father to us all. Not long after that afternoon on the Column, Ron climbed his way across Europe, then onto the Karakoram and beyond, closing the circle on the traditional era of rock climbing. But I couldn't call him now.

Too anxious to sleep, turning this last pitch over in my mind like a pig on a spit, I'd fairly dragged Ron and John out of their sleeping bags, then had burgled the two leads up to this crumbly face. Now I couldn't muster the sack to pull a single move.

I hated this situation. I loved it, too. Not a soul, not even God, stood between me and the decision I faced. Do or fly. The moment my feet left that pillar, my life would change forever.

Gritting my teeth and fingering those useless pitons, I peered up at the flaky holds, shifting foot to foot on my tiny stance. It felt like the route was taunting me, playing my ego off itself so I'd lose patience, crank into something stupid, and plummet terribly as the whole Valley howled.

But fuck it. There were holds, and I only had 25 feet to go. Maybe less. I glanced left and growled, "Here goes." Then I blanked my mind and pulled off the pinnacle.

After a body length, it felt unlikely I could reverse any of this, so I accepted that I was basically soloing. Strangely, I relaxed. If this was what the route demanded, I'd go with it. The climbing wasn't nearly so hard as I was making it. Scared as I was of snapping an edge, I cranked a series of screwball twisty moves to avoid reefing too hard on suspect handholds and keep some weight over the granular footholds.

After about ten feet, I stretched high off a flexing carbuncle and pinched the bottom of a big grimy tongue drooping down, clasping both sides in turn, anxiously wiggling a few sketchy wired nuts into the flaring grain. The only pins I had that would fit behind the tongue were bashed into that seam below.

Fifteen feet to go.

Bear-hugging like mad, I gunned for the roof, feet bicycling the choss. Grains rained down. The tongue flexed and groaned. My eyes zeroed in on the short hand crack extending down from the roof, but after a few more bear hugs, I'd only reached a sloping sandbar, which I'd have to straight mantel to stretch a hand into the crack.

This was bullshit. If I blew off here, I'd go for a monster whipper and probably hit the ledge. I hated this route with all my heart. Piece of shit goddamn garbage wall from hell! *What the fuck?*

"What's going on over there?" Ron yelled from around the corner.

"Just watch me," I yelled back.

"We can't even see you," said Bachar.

"Just watch the damn rope," I said.

I splayed my feet, soles flush on the crud, one hand pawing the tongue as I raked the sandy berm, trying to get down to solid rock. Cocking into a mantel at last, I pressed it out like molasses, gingerly placing a foot on the crunchy veneer and stepping up with my teeth chattering and no handholds. Finally, I could stretch up to the crack, sink a hand jam, and slot a bomber hex.

I leaned back off the jam and gazed down at the pitiful wires bristling from the tongue and the loose face, patted with chalk marks, plunging to the tied-off pegs. The wicked hard climbing I feared never came, the real challenge being the crap rock. Uncertainty, again, had lit my mind on fire.

All told, this was like the best pitch I'd ever done. Perfect, really. And beneath the pinnacle, diving 1,200 undercut feet straight into the talus — a face of wonders. I felt like the Valley's favored son. Reaching out over the roof, I could just clasp a good, flat-top hold. I pulled up and realized my hands were on top of Washington Column.

We called it *Astroman*. Following an early ascent, the British ace Pete Livesey called it "the world's greatest free climb," a title that stuck for the next twenty-something years. During that time, the last pitch, "the sting in the tail," cleaned up nicely following a thorough brushing and hundreds of ascents. Several long, thin pitons were welded behind the tongue, as well as some copper-heads. But the caveat for the last pitch remains the same as it did in July 1975: *Don't fall.*

EL CAP AND HALF DOME IN A DAY

Peter Croft

From *The Valley Climbers*

Off the rock, John stumbled and bumbled through the same mine fields we all face. But at the right intersection of vision and action, John Bachar's best moments were mountainous.

A few hundred yards from the basalt bluff where I started climbing I found a geological anomaly: a dark grey and white granite globe, weighing perhaps 100 pounds, nestled amidst a jumbled black scree field. Even then the magnetic mythology of Yosemite granite compelled me to act rashly, and I spent hours stumbling and wrestling the precious piebald stone to the base of my practice bluff.

Yosemite has had this enchanting effect on thousands of climbers. To the outsider it must seem odd that meadows, trees, and magical rocks, fitted into a mile-wide ditch with a river running through it, could focus the energies of feral boys and girls and charm them into the Valley and onto dangerous ascents. From the inside, of course, the long drive down from a cold Canada was a crusade. When we'd stop in Manteca for gas and Doritos, we all accepted the shimmering heat as coming from the center of the universe.

Enchainments

The idea of link ups, or "enchainments," was not new, but in my case was mostly limited to solo adventures on the smaller walls like Sentinel, the Cathedrals, North Dome, and so forth, the challenge being how many of these formations I could tuck into a day. But year after year as I topped out on the various points along the rim it became impossible to ignore the bald faced enormities of El Cap and Half Dome.

I clearly remember that early summer's day in 1986 when I met John Bachar. Fresh out of the Canadian winter and stale from the 24 hours of beelining it to Yosemite, my friends and I postponed setting up camp and instead stopped at the first crag we came to: Reed's Pinnacle.

I'd come to the Valley single minded. For two years I'd obsessed over the idea of linking El Cap and Half Dome. To those I'd blurted my plan, I was deranged. What I needed was the perfect partner — namely John — but the crushing awe he inspired held me back. Too shy to approach him, I needed some lucky confluence of events to throw us together. I wanted a miracle. As it happened, I was digging for a chalk bag and shoes when John's black Forerunner swept into the turn out.

John jumped onto the pavement and my head dropped deferentially — I couldn't help it. Here was climbing royalty. He strode right up and asked if I wanted to go soloing. Stunned, I stammered "Y-y-y-yes."

In a quick minute we were scrambling up through bay trees and boulders towards the base of the cliff. As soon as we were out of earshot of the others he fired the question: "You wanna do El Cap and Half Dome?" At that point the walls could have fallen to the Valley floor and I wouldn't have heard a thing. It is the closest I've ever felt to the divine taking a personal interest in my little world.

The Greatest Climber in the World

Today it's unfashionable to use superlatives like "hero." I'm not sure why. Maybe because when we draw in close, we see all the rust on the shield. Even Alexander wasn't Great all the time, it is true, and off the rock, John stumbled and bumbled through the same mine fields we all face. But at the right intersection of vision and action, John Bachar's best moments were mountainous.

John's legend was richer and more exotic than sound bytes and anecdotes in magazines. His aura swelled with the frightening stories about his solos whispered in the dusty Camp 4 parking lot, or when someone pointed out Midnight Lightning, that world-famous nugget of overhanging rock, where Bachar had been running laps for seasons on end. We all can still picture John cranking one-arms for 100 feet to the summit of the absurdly tall Bachar ladder hanging off the lip of Cyclops Rock in Joshua Tree. Under the weight of all that lore I heeded his advice. "Two full rest days," he said sternly. Wide-eyed I nodded but inwardly I flinched, sure I would fall out of shape. "Eat as much as you can," seemed to compound the problem, as now I'd be getting weak and fat.

The Captain

When we stood in the dark at the base of El Cap, however, it was as he had foretold — the fuse had been lit! Pitches glided out of our headlamp beams and we tiptoed past snoring climbers, clutching gear against our legs so we wouldn't wake them.

It got light around Boot Flake, and I had just followed the King Swing when John asked about the tag line. A horrified look down confirmed the worst. I had no idea how — but the line was gone. John was unperturbed. "Okay, this'll still work. Don't worry about it." With a word or a look he could easily have twisted the knife in my embarrassment, but he was already flashing upwards as he joked about people still eating breakfast at the cafeteria.

We were not swinging leads, rather each man would lead half a dozen pitches in a row before we'd switch over. As I swung into the lead a couple pitches above Camp Six, I jumped up and grabbed a man-sized block. The block teetered on its perch and my world spun nightmarishly backwards.

Several things happened spontaneously. I released the block and leapt, aiming at tiny landing while freaking about a chunk of granite busting into pieces and ricocheting down the upper dihedrals below. Just an hour earlier we had passed five climbers.

Mid-jump, I caught a blur of color in my peripheral vision. It was John, lunging forward to shove the block back into place, a Superman moment but in real life. Once again, he would hear none of my apologies, muttering something like, "That flake was so ready to go."

We pressed on, up the perfect finger and hand cracks to the overhanging last pitch, which hangs like a brow over the very bridge of The Nose. Coiling the rope on top, the spark we began with had ignited a firestorm of momentum and we blazed to the East Ledges and down the rappels, hitting the ground at a jog.

The Dome

By the time we got to Half Dome storm clouds were already mushrooming over the high country, but the dark threat merely added fuel to our fire. The route follows several thousand feet of corner cracks — the result of the dome scaling away like an exfoliating onion — and right off we started simul-climbing. There were lots of climbers on the face, and in three separate places I wasn't allowed past until John showed up. Without a trace of arrogance, his face conjured deference from the slack jawed and, thanks to the rope, allowed both of us to blast on.

Once, though, at a hanging stance, the belayer more or less bowed to John, but when the rope ran out and I tried to pass, he leaned out mightily to block my path. Unable to jam the crack, I turned to wild stemming on the outer reaches of the corner. Then, as planets aligned, he leaned out even further as I made a blind foot dyno, the stiffness of my board lasted shoe making a loud thwack as it contacted his skull. I apologized, but felt as though I'd just kicked a goal for John.

Three-quarters of the way up the wall, I pulled onto Big Sandy ledges and three big Germans eating lunch. On hearing that John Bachar was coming up right behind them, they dropped their knackwurst, rushed out to the edge, and strained off their leashes, their greasy fingers clawing the air to get a better view.

The storm finally hit. Coiled static did squirrely things with our hair and jabbed our neck and hands with pins and needles. The cliff glistened and rivulets ran. But even the rain and crackling buzz of lightning couldn't douse the flame and slow our trajectory. Late that afternoon, we crested the summit to a double rainbow.

THE SALATHÉ FREE

Paul Piana

From the *American Alpine Journal*, 1989

A piece of dropped gear fell for over twenty seconds before vanishing in the void. Todd was later quoted as saying you get so high up on El Cap it takes five minutes to see the ground.

In September of 1961, Yosemite wall pioneers Tom Frost, Chuck Pratt and Royal Robbins established the second route up the great face of El Capitan. The Salathé Wall crossed all known frontiers in technical difficulty, and for many years afterwards was promoted as "The Greatest Rock Climb in the World."

More than a generation later, the goal of leading climbers was no longer to merely climb the route, but rather to free climb to the summit. Todd Skinner and I were free-climbers, and we considered the Salathé the greatest free-climbing prize in the world. There was nothing remotely as grand or sustained in difficulty. From Todd's reconnaissances in 1985 and 1987, it was obvious we couldn't begin to free-climb the Salathé without a lot of preparation.

Our eventual strategy involved spending six or seven days at time on a kind of vertical camping trip, working on discrete sections of the wall. We never had free climbed in such a fantastically exposed place. We marveled how at each impasse we discovered a workable sequence, even if just barely. Still, we were astonished by the inhuman amount of difficult climbing we faced. Following a month of recons and armed with a photo team and several weeks' worth of food and water, we cast off for an all-out ground-up push. We figured we just might succeed if we could somehow avoid injury, and if the weather stayed cool and dry.

Ten rope-lengths of intricate slab climbing, first freed in 1975, lead to Heart Ledges, followed by 600 feet of spectacular cracks to a hanging belay beneath the first extreme pitch. Were it on the ground, this 5.13b dihedral would be a much-tried classic, but the 1,700-foot approach will deter many. Power flares into pin scars and back out again, then thuggish laybacking all led to the hard part—searing fingertip pin scars, laser-precise edging, and post-doctoral body English over the last twenty feet.

By way of vigorous stemming and wild slaps, Todd flashed a desperate polished corner two rope-lengths above El Cap Spire. Soon the Headwall loomed over us like a dark cloud. The pitch below the jutting roof required strenuous, open-hand lay backing and grim stemming protected by a string of frayed bashies. Don't fall. This flaring dihedral ended at a dangling stance nearing the

2,500 foot level and just below the Great Roof—a bold feature that stair-steps over and out for twenty feet and onto the chilling headwall above. The walls of the corner below cocooned us from the wind, so we hauled our bags and set up our portaledge camp.

Ropes, gear, and our very lives were tangled across the hanging corner like a giant cobweb. Our little world was secure, but we could never truly relax. The position was simply too shocking. A piece of dropped gear fell for over twenty seconds before vanishing in the void. Todd was later quoted as saying you get so high up on El Cap it takes five minutes to see the ground.

From the top floor of our camp, with acres of morning beneath my heels, I pumped out right along an easy but spectacular traverse that found a series of dead-point surges to sloping buckets. From here I moved wildly to the right, feet swinging, then threw my leg up and over a huge horizontal spike. What a place! Halfway out a massive roof, 100 miles off the deck, was this amazing saddle-like peninsula so flat and comfortable that I could have served coffee on it. From the saddle, it's all rounded buckets to the lip and a terrifying heel-toe above the head and crank to a shoulder scum. All the while, my heart was slugging away while I made the tenuous step up onto a hands-down rest. We decided to throw in a belay here since we had the stance.

The 5.12+ flare moves just off the belay were the hardest jamming moves we had ever experienced, and were unprotected as well. With his shoes fifteen unprotected feet above the anchor, Todd desperately pulled up slack to clip a tied-off peg. The slightest error would have sent him screaming off and over the roof till he crashed onto my belay anchors, wild-eyed and spinning thousands of feet off the ground. We were both glad he didn't rip. The flare ended with a short but wicked face sequence. We were ecstatic that the second 5.13 pitch was done, but sobered because two more stretched above.

The headwall's two 5.13 jamming pitches follow a stupendous crack splitting the 100° sweep of golden granite near the zenith of EI Capitan. Todd called the first lead "the most beautiful pitch I've ever seen," surely in the most impressive location imaginable. The pitch was so strenuous that to succeed you had to run it out rather than waste energy placing pro. Twice I thought Todd had it, only to pitch off a move shy of the anchor. Against all hope, Todd went up a last time, fighting upward with violent karate-chop jamming, frantic foot changes and missed clips. Then 90 feet up, a dejected murmur and I was yanked upward as Todd once more hit the end of the rope.

We both were physically and emotionally shot. Our knuckles had swollen to a shocking size and our hands no longer closed. We simply didn't have the rations to hang around and recover. The next morning Todd mumbled that he needed a rest day. Instead, we jumared our photographer's ropes to the pitch that exited onto Long Ledge. I could almost get this pitch but every time would fail a few feet short. I must have fallen a nautical mile that day, but we gained valuable knowledge about subtle foot placements, and Todd did get a little rest as a belay slave. Even so, my gobied fingers were oozing horribly through the superglue and tape. We retreated to our hanging camp and worked at repairing my fingers. I tried to relax and sleep, but couldn't. I climbed that Long Ledge exit pitch a thousand times in my mind while the cool void tingled in the darkness below.

Next morning we spent several hours eating breakfasts, and finally started up the fixed lines to do battle with the headwall. Straightaway Todd climbed fifteen feet above the top pro, and dramatically jumped into the void. He repeated this several times until his reluctance to go for it was completely gone. The sun hadn't hit the face, and the winds on the headwall had died off. Todd flowed through the stillness, slowing at the last few moves, taking care to climb flawlessly. And then all was laughter as he clipped the belay and I started up to join him.

Todd and I spent an hour cleaning my hands with alcohol, supergluing the rents in my fingers and then carefully applying a wrap of tape over the glue. Before starting, I torqued my fingers in the crack to numb the pain. The morning's lethargy became adrenalin as the thin jams were suddenly below and I found myself wedged into a pod-like slot. Exiting the slot seemed particularly rude to my tattered hands, the flared jams as painful as backhanding a wire brush. After clipping the highest piece, I found myself staring at the dyno target. Todd was screaming, "Hit it! Hit it!" Long seconds passed. A deliberate lunge and I pinched the knob and cranked to the belay, laughing and waving my arms like a lunatic.

We rappelled down the headwall and under the roof,

packed our gear and slowly hauled it to Long Ledge. After the freight-hauling, we had a little daylight left and were hungry for the top.

The pitch off Long Ledge is a face-climbing continuation of the headwall, and rolls and bulges upward. Todd reveled in the delicate foot changes, long reaches between knobs and dead-points to crisp side pulls. Inspired by the summit so near, he danced up this pocketed wonder, then I dashed up a superb 5.10 hand crack that placed us one pitch from the top. Todd made light work of the last bit of 5.11 and the Free Salathé was done.

The next morning we breakfasted and started hauling freight to the rim. I was first over the top and lashed us off to a huge block, the same one used by years of Salathé climbers. Soon, Todd reached the rim, and while he heaved up the extra ropes, I cleaned the anchor and turned to lift the haul bags. At the sound of a horrible grating noise we spun round to see that the giant anchor block had come loose and was sliding toward the lip.

The rest is vague. I recall the two of us being battered together and the horror of seeing my partner pitched wildly off the edge, and then feeling a tremendous weight on my left leg as I was squeegied off the rim. There was a loud crack like a rifle shot, more pummeling and suddenly everything stopped spinning and I could just peek back over the edge. Everything was in tatters—ropes pinched off and fused and cut in various places. I was afraid to touch anything, and sick with the knowledge that Todd had just taken the big ride into the deck. Then a startling bass squeak sounded below me, followed by a desperate, "Grab the rope!"

I handwalked the rope over the top and soon a bloody hand on a crushed ascender slid over the rim. I helped Todd up and we lay there for a long time. We were terrified because Todd was having trouble breathing and his pelvis hurt badly. My leg was in a weird position and reaching a crescendo of pain.

I don't know how long we were there, afraid to move for fear of unraveling the braid of cut ropes that miraculously held us. When we did get up, we discovered that Todd's line appeared to be okay. He had been held by one of his ascenders. Apparently the block had scraped over the ascender, and miraculously that small, gouged, and bent piece of metal had kept Todd's rope from being cut. I had been saved by the loop I'd casually clipped to a fixed pin next to the block. The 11 mm rope tied into the block had been cut as easily as a cotton shoelace. Two other 9 mm ropes were in eight or nine pieces, and the haul bags had whistled 3,200 feet to the talus. We coiled the remaining rope and staggered down the East Ledges. In our broken state, a descent that usually took under two hours required almost seven.

We had dreamed, we had trained, and we had struggled. Even though the climb ended with a nightmare, we had triumphed because we were prepared to fail and fail and fail until we could succeed. The Free Salathé is unrelenting and the logistics are staggering. Perhaps once again, this time as a super free route, the Salathé Wall is once again "the world's greatest rock climb."

FREEING THE NOSE IN ONE DAY (1994)

Lynn Hill

From *The Valley Climbers*

It took me years to fully digest what took place on that magical September day, when according to Alpinist Magazine, "The modern era was born."

During one of my visits back to California in the early nineties I met with my old friend John Long. "Lynnie, you should try making the first free ascent of the Nose on El Cap," he said. "It's one of the last great problems in American free climbing." Of course! After years of climbing competitions in Europe, here at last was a big, natural challenge that would require all the skills, experience and values that defined my life as a climber. Whether I succeeded or not, the Nose free was a goal worthy of my best effort.

The Nose of El Capitan is one of the world's most famous big walls. Ever since Warren Harding's first ascent in 1958, the route has remained a benchmark to set and measure standards. The first one-day ascent in 1975 set a precedent for speed; by 1992, climbers whittled the time down from fifteen hours to an incredible four hours and twenty two minutes. By then, much of the route went free, and for several years the push was on to free-climb the entire route, bottom to top. However a few sections had stopped all comers cold. My decades of experience in traditional-style climbing, plus my six years of performing on the international competition circuit, gave me the confidence to believe in my chances. When I headed up El Cap on my first attempt to free the Nose, it felt like coming home.

Some twenty years had passed since I first visited Yosemite with my family and saw this grand granite monolith. The Nose had later been a rite of passage when Mari Gingery, Dean Fidelman and I struggled up the wall in 1979, climbing the route mostly on aid during our three day ascent. Thirteen years later I logged a speed ascent with Hans Florine, in just over eight hours. At thirty-three, and spread out over several weeks — first with Simon Nadine, and finally with Brooke Sandahl — I managed to free-climb the Nose during a four day push in September, 1993. Though significant, this ascent was merely a prelude for a much greater challenge: to free-climb the Nose in one day.

Planning on a mid-summer ascent, I started training in early spring. I ran and climbed almost daily, ratcheting up the intensity every week. I needed high endurance because the most difficult sections begin after nearly 2,000 feet of climbing. Through my practice of trying to go as far as possible while expending the least energy, I discovered a higher level of consciousness in my climbing.

I knew that free-climbing the Nose in one marathon push would require a huge effort, but I underestimated the complexities, which included organizing a film team to document the effort. As on most big walls, anything that could go wrong, did go wrong. But I made an effort to remain patient and relaxed no matter what the situation presented, reminding myself, "It's all part of the climb."

Nevertheless I was exhausted by the time I finally roped up. My only constant was my climbing partner, Steve Sutton, a longtime friend and big wall veteran capable of following each pitch at breakneck speed while carrying all our food, water, and supplies in a small daypack.

We started up the Nose on a hot August day, 1994. Twenty-two pitches later we hung in slings beneath the Great Roof, one of the most difficult pitches on the route. I had run out of chalk, we were nearly out of water, and the intense mid-day heat had sapped my energy. After five attempts spread over five and a half hours, I still hadn't free climbed the Great Roof. At 6:00 p.m. I abandoned my all-free ascent. By the time we reached the summit at 9:00 p.m. I was so thrashed that I questioned my chances of ever free-climbing the Nose in a day. But despite my discouragement, I didn't abandon the dream.

On September 19 at 10:00 p.m. we started up the Nose once more. Under the light of a full moon, Steve and I climbed pitch after pitch through the still night. Arriving at Camp Four at 8:30 a.m., I dozed off for what seemed like ten minutes and woke suddenly as the sun rounded the corner of the soaring South Buttress. I had to start climbing while it remained cool under the Great Roof.

The previous year, following 40 feet of desperate, fingertip laybacking, I finally gained the roof itself. Ducking my head inside the curl of this granite wave, I could just wedge two fingers tips of each hand straight up into the crack, as my feet pressed flat against the holdless, vertical wall. Setting this rock-surfing posture into motion involved tendon-popping finger stabs and delicate tai-chi like foot shuffles. After trying countless hand and foot sequences, my strength and concentration were nearly spent. I knew I could free-climb this pitch, but I wasn't sure I had the strength to do it that day.

This time I powered up the lower section without pause, but felt maxed the moment I plugged into the roof. After ten feet I knew I could make it only if I kept moving, so I skipped a key piece of protection out in the middle and gunned it for the belay, risking a generous whipper. Toward the end of the roof traverse my foot suddenly skated off and I nearly fell, but my head butted into the ceiling above me, unexpectedly giving me a point of balance. I smeared my feet onto rounded bumps, extended my right arm and stuffed my fingertips into a small slot. A few moves later, at 10:25 a.m., I clipped the belay bolts, having redpointed the Great Roof on my first try.

But more difficult climbing loomed overhead. I began the notorious Glowering Spot pitch at high noon, during peak heat. Below the crux I slotted a wired stopper; just as I launched into the 5.12 moves the crucial stopper slid from the crack and rattled down the rope. Facing a possible ledge fall, pushing further was dangerous, but trying to down climb almost certainly meant forfeiting my no-falls ascent. Fortunately, I managed to slot one of my last pieces of gear, then ran the rope to the belay.

An hour later Steve and I were hunkered below the Changing Corners pitch, the technical crux of the route. The rock was too hot for free-climbing, so we stopped at Camp Six. We both were exhausted. Now over 2,500 feet above the ground, it seemed as though gravity increased the higher we climbed. Having studied Chi Gong with a Chinese master a few months prior, I imagined a powerful energy source flowing up through the rock and extending beyond the summit toward infinity. I felt this ascent was tied to my destiny and that I could somehow tap that mysterious energy, much greater than my own, and rise upward in its current. By 5:30 p.m., most of the pitch was bathed in shade and I was anxious to give it a go.

To free-climb the Changing Corners I had pieced together a wild tango of smears, tenuous stems, back steps, cross steps, lay backs, arm bars, pinches, and palming maneuvers unlike anything I'd ever done before. The crux itself, which Brooke Sandahl coined the "Houdini Move," involved a bizarre contortion as unlikely as a disappearing act, where I managed spin 180 degrees in the shallow corner. Now, as I launched into the first difficult moves, with my arms outstretched in an iron-cross and my feet splayed on vague dents, I could feel my boots beginning to butter off. The rock was still too hot. I desperately matched hands on the inside corner of the smooth arête, then wedged my fingertips into the tiny crack and pivoted my body around into the corner. Soon as I began working my fingertips higher, I pinged off and dropped onto the rope. This was my first fall on the route, and I was disappointed to have muffed my no-falls ascent. I rested at the belay for twenty minutes, then fell again on my second attempt. As I began the opening moves on my third try, my foot slipped off during the second move. Afraid that my free ascent might be foiled once more, I needed to rest and adjust my attitude before giving it one last shot.

I glanced out across the valley to Middle Cathedral and saw once more the heart-shaped shadow that the previous year helped inspire my successful ascent of the Great Roof. The shadow line had risen up the wall, underlining the point of the heart, that timeless badge of love and ultimately, the motivation behind my greatest achievements. No woman, and possibly no man, had ever done such a significant first free ascent in Yosemite Valley. Ever since childhood when guys would say, "Gee, I can't even do that!" or later in life when people said, "It's not possible," I became even keener to demonstrate what is possible with an open mind and heart. And now was the ideal moment to give the Changing Corners my last full-hearted effort.

If I should ever free-climb the Nose of El Capitan, it would almost certainly boil down to the next few minutes. Since impatience had already cost me dearly, it was critical not to rush the full-twisting "Houdini" move. This time the sequences flowed together and I was ecstatic to finally make it on what surely was my final try. Free-climbing this pitch in such an exhausted state had required a greater effort than any climb I had ever done before.

Just as night fell we pulled beneath the summit overhangs and the last strenuous pitch of 5.12c. My muscles felt slow and heavy. Clicking on my headlamp, I reached out to the edge of a bulge just above. When I latched this hold and let my feet swing out I felt an alarming fatigue in my arms. I focused on a tiny edge on the face above, lunged upward and caught the edge with two fingertips. More hard moves rushed at me out of the night. At the final overhang I was so gassed I had to leap for a hold, hit-or-miss style. The dwindling electricity of my headlamp matched the fading strength of my arms. I pulled over the summit after 23 hours of climbing.

Jim Bridwell and Hugh Burton met us on top, their headlamps shining a path out into the night. My mind swirled in an otherworldly state, yet under the bright stars, I felt peaceful and serine. In my dream-like trance I could not possibly comprehend all that I had just experienced, how my entire life had converged into this climb. In fact, it took me years to fully digest what took place on that magical September day, when according to Alpinist magazine, "The modern era was born."

ADEMDUM

I never imagined that 25 years after first free climbing the Nose, I would return with a talented young Swiss climber named Nina Caprez. My intention was to support

Nina's effort to free climb the route, while celebrating the 25th anniversary of the first free ascent. Repeating an all free ascent of the Nose would have certainly been ideal, but my expectations were tempered by family life and juggling various work commitments. After watching images of myself free climbing the crux pitches on the Nose with apparent ease over the years, I actually believed that this route wasn't so hard! My perspective completely changed after my experiences with Nina in 2018 and 2019! I still find it hard to believe that over 30 years later, Tommy Caldwell and I are the only ones to have made an all free ascent of the Nose in one day!

In the years since, it has given me great satisfaction to see other climbers expanding the possibilities of free climbing on the big walls in Yosemite. Several more free ascents of other routes on El Cap have been done by numerous climbers from the U.S. and around the world. I'm particularly happy to see so many amazing women making impressive free ascents on the big walls of Yosemite and other more remote big walls around the world. Revisiting the Nose in 2018 and 2019 reminded me of how hard it really was to free climb those crux pitches and how much power can be accessed with the right attitude and motivation. Though Nina literally fell only one inch short of an all free ascent of the Nose, this fact did not define or negate her experiences. In fact, this turned out to be a life changing experience for Nina, which ultimately led to meeting her life partner and having their daughter, Lia. Climbing and the relationships that develop through shared experiences, have also provided the most valuable lessons and the greatest meaning in my life.

SOLOING THE LINK-UP (1998)

Hans Florine

From *The Valley Climbers*

I can't sleep, so I pace a trench in the floor of my Yosemite cabin. In a few hours I will try and become the first person to solo the renowned "link-up," climbing the Regular Route on Half Dome and the Nose on El Capitan in one day. If somehow I can pull this off, I'll have a first for the ages. More likely I'll go down in flames. Either way I'm going for it. I pace some more.

It's 10:00 p.m. in my Yosemite cabin. In a few hours I will try and become the first person to rope solo the renowned "link-up," climbing the Regular Route on Half Dome and the Nose on El Capitan, both in one day. If somehow I can pull this off I'll have a first for the ages. More likely I'll go down in flames. Either way I'm going for it. There's a calm comfort in that knowledge. I close my eyes and drift off, gliding over a sea of granite.

At 3:24 the next morning, July 28, 1998, I start out from the Stables parking lot, accompanied by my South African friend, Alard Hüfner, along to shoot pictures and video. An hour and 49 minutes of hiking gains the base of Half Dome. The spring is flowing and it's a blessing to drink my fill before casting off. I rest a bit, rack my gear and at 5:47 a.m. I'm good to go.

The previous June, Dean Potter rope soloed the Regular Route in a remarkable 4 hours and 17 minutes. Later that winter I got wind that Dean was considering a rope solo attempt on the link-up, the historic "enchainment" first achieved by John Bachar and Peter Croft in 1986. Over the last decade the link-up had been repeated by only four teams, and never solo. As I peer up at 2,000 feet of vertical granite, the venture feels surreal.

When my hands finally touch rock I stop thinking, drop into physical meditation and quietly watch my limbs carry me skywards. Concerns about an outcome and the earth itself drop away as my life narrows to the next move, and the next one after that.

I free solo (no rope) the first pitch, rope solo a full 60 meter length, then rope solo a bolt ladder followed by a 5.9 hand crack. I ascend past a German team also climbing the route in a day — they must have started in the dark, with headlamps. I free solo to the bolt ladder at the Robbins Traverse, then rappel and rope solo to the base of the long chimneys.

Roughly at the halfway mark, a thousand feet up the wall, I'm amazed to arrive here more than an hour faster than during my previous run a few weeks earlier, when to gain vital reconnaissance, I'd free and roped soloed the route in just under seven hours. Taking nearly double the time Dean required proved what I already knew — that

Dean Potter is a monster talent. It also spelled disaster for my link-up plans.

I needed at least two hours to descend Half Dome and get to the base of El Capitan, leaving me only fourteen hours to climb the Nose. Sure, several years ago I rope soloed the Nose in fourteen hours, but not just after soloing a 2,000-foot big wall and jogging five miles. Last night my goal felt like a longshot. Now, halfway up the Dome, I am beginning to like my chances.

After 60 meters of rope soloing up the chimneys I'm briefly free of leading, rappelling, and cleaning my gear, and quickly free solo up to Big Sandy ledges. I rope solo up the super-exposed Zig-Zags, to the right side of Thank God Ledge, then solo off, "roping in" twice by leaving two leaver biners on bolts that I pull past till finally I'm paddling over the summit blocks and stop the watch at 3:53, fairly amazed to have shaved nearly three hours off my previous time. Jammed alongside a knot of hikers on top, Alard is out on the summit visor, shooting video. It is not yet 10:00 a.m. For a moment I share the summit with scores of strangers. I must have felt something, had a moment's pause or reflective interlude. But so briefly were these things experienced they are totally lost on me now, consumed as I was on maintaining speed and saving time.

We dash down the cables on the back side of the Dome, beat it back to the base, stuff my gear in the day pack and shoot down the slabs. Along the way I wolf down a banana, apricots, and a protein bar, then stop at the Lodge store for ice cream. I am keenly aware of the ticking clock but know that an ice cream break is needed to catch a second wind for the Captain. We get in the car and gun it down the loop road for El Cap Meadow.

Many things have changed in climbing, but the greatest honor still goes to the climber who is first — be it a first ascent, a first free ascent, a first solo ascent, or a first one day ascent.

From the moment I heard of Dean's proposal to solo the link up, I knew that here was an almost mythical first I could hang my hopes on, a crowning achievement for my climbing and athletic career. And as we pull over at the El Cap turnout to meet my friend and partner, Steve Schneider, I'm thrilled to be ahead of schedule.

As I gush about bagging the solo record on Half Dome, Steve's face suddenly goes dark. After a deadpan, "Good job," Steve informs me that Dean Potter had unexpectedly flown in from Colorado and sent the solo link-up, yesterday. "Rad. Awesome!" I blurt. But after a few moments the immensity of my disillusionment rips the wind out of me and I keep murmuring, "I'm not going to be first. I'm not going to be first." Steve tries to rally me, but I'm in a tailspin, unsure how to process such deflating news.

The essence of the goal I had dreamed about, visualized, and incessantly trained for has empowered me since two o'clock this morning. Now it seems glory has been yanked away. I cannot just stand there on the side of the road, empty handed. I must take an action. Months of programming can only push me in one direction, and glumly, robotically, I tromp off for El Cap. It feels like heading to the rock pile on Monday morning. I have roughly 17.5 hours left before my 24 hours run out. So off I go . . . to work.

I rope solo up to Sickle Ledge in two long pitches, rap over to the Dolt Hole cracks, then anchor and rope solo into the Stove Legs for 60 meters. I'm pissed, I'm pathetic, I'm all shook up. But I'm also pumping up one of the finest granite walls in creation. Really now, how could soloing the link-up be anything but sweet, this pure Tom Sawyer exuberance of flowing up the Big Stone. I almost laugh out loud. I am right where I need to be.

When I sweep past Camp Four and the halfway point, my watch says six hours have elapsed. One more push takes me to the triangle ledge after Pancake Flake. Darkness falls, I don my headlamp and pull for Camp 5, 2,200 feet up the face. I so much want to nod off on the comfy ledge, but a friend is bivouacked there and he urges me on. I punch up to the Glowering Spot, then on to Camp 6. My body is running on fumes and my mind indifferently observes the moves made, the protection placed, the ascenders fastened to a rope snaking up into night. Round about midnight I nearly trip over my friend Mark Wellman, sleeping in his bag. Mark is paralyzed from the waist down but this hasn't stopped him from completing his second lap up El Capitan — an inspiring performance for sure. Mark knows what I'm up to and he mentions that Dean Potter was through the night before doing the same damn thing. We laugh and share a drink, two climbers high in the moon-lit corners of El Capitan.

Several months ago, in my normal forward style, I

publicly announced that I would attempt the solo link-up today. In fact broadcasting my plans was like screaming from the dark. Sure, there's a wonky kid part of me always jumping around and yelling, "Look at me! Look what I can do!" But secretly I wanted friends to talk sense into me lest I became the first climber to fail at the solo link-up. The adventure could never be remotely safe, I'd have to climb myself to smithereens to even get close, and my doubts only multiplied as I marched into July. Strangely, not a single friend balked at my plans, rather they all encouraged me wholeheartedly. And it was the unwavering faith of friends that finally put me "all in."

Leaving Mark at Camp Six I push past the Changing Corners anchor, then to the final belay below the Alcove. Only a final 5.10 crack and the overhanging bolt ladder lay overhead. It is approaching 2 AM. Clipping up the bolt ladder I can hear Alard and Abby Watkins hooting for me on top; their voices are like magnets, drawing me upward.

I pull over the summit utterly smashed, and embrace my two friends. After the first few pitches, and for the thousands of feet of climbing that followed, it had never entered my mind that I wouldn't be first to solo the link-up, probably because there is no second place on the Captain.

EL NIÑO: FREEING THE NORTH AMERICAN WALL (1998)

Thomas Huber

From *The Valley Climbers*

The rope slowly pays out. All I can do is wait — wait for him to come flying over the roof, or wait for his cry of relief when he reaches the anchors. He screams. He's got the belay bolts. That son of a bitch has nerves of steel.

1998. We sit in the meadow and stare up at the towering granite bulk of El Capitan, a ritual we have done many times before. Virtually all of El Cap's many faces have fallen to free climbers: The West Face, The Salathé Wall, The Nose, and the East Buttress. But what about the Southeast Face? Dark and foreboding, the largely overhanging wall hosts a dense grid of extreme aid routes. In 1964, the only passage followed the legendary North America Wall, long hailed as the toughest wall climb in the world. An aid climbing milestone in its day, the "NA" now offered itself as a radical free-climbing prospect, owing to the richly-featured diorite rock covering much of the Southeast Face.

Alexander zooms in with the telescope, comparing our tentative plans with the visible flakes, dikes, and crack systems he could spot through the glass. Alpinist Conrad Anker has provided vital information on the wall. When we inquired about the NA, he pulled out a secret topo map of a potential free line he had only just found the previous week. A free line here is at once a bold and brilliant notion, for this is the steepest wall on all of El Capitan. Even with our telescope and Conrad's hand drawn treasure map, many questions remain. Is there really a free route between the first hold on the first pitch and the last hold on the last pitch? We have traveled here from Germany to find out.

Wasting no time, we organize gear and drag our heavy packs to the foot of the wall. It is always magical to place both hands on El Cap after a prolonged separation. I tilt my head back and follow the line of all my dreams, wishing myself nearly 1,000 meters above, a point that feels unattainable. But it is exactly this uncertainty that stirs our desires and dares us to risk this adventure.

The objective is not so much to free a particular route as it is to discover a free route up the entire Southeast Face. Wherever the holds lead us, that's where we will go. The Footstool — a small, pointed buttress at the start of New Jersey Turnpike — seems the best place to start. We spend half a day on the route, only to have it dead end. Conrad's topo suggests an alternative line to the left. Looking across I can see the thick, diorite vein, called the Black Dike, cutting through otherwise featureless golden granite. Conrad has already climbed this pitch and placed some bolts.

We return the next morning and find the easiest way through the Black Dike is still 5.13b. The next challenge, linking the Black Dike and the Galapagos, involves a smooth patch just off the belay, with tantalizing chickenheads a few body lengths above. When the only feature, a small flake, breaks under my fingers, it seems we have dead-ended once more. Then I notice that the subsequent scar has left a tiny edge — just enough to make progress. The two-millimeter wide detail has opened a 900 meter passageway. The Galapagos, a very severe face, brings us back to New Jersey Turnpike and the toughest pitch yet. This completes Conrad's variation. It cost us enormous energy to climb, but it goes and the first stage is conquered. Five hundred meters to go.

We plan to spend the next five days on the face, hoping to free-climb through the middle section of North America Wall. The next 150 meters will feature the most exciting and potentially difficult sections of our mission: the notorious "Slingshot Traverse," a jumbo pendulum immortalized in books and magazines, and the huge and enormously exposed roof of the Black Cave.

The climbing up to the bivouac site on Big Sur gives us few problems. By evening, we are settled with all our gear on the long meter-wide ledge. We are now on the west coast of the massive diorite intrusion, easily 1,000 feet across, that describes the shape of the North American continent from which the route derived its name. So far, so good.

By first light the next morning we can see the sparkling

granite of the Pacific out left, as well as our next obstacles: the two pendulum traverses which hopefully will lead to the Black Dihedral. We manage with difficulty to free the first pendulum. On the second traverse, however, there simply are no holds that might link us to the dihedral. We search up, down, and around, but all in vain. The path beyond is blocked. Our hopes are dashed.

Working out a free route on El Capitan is still a novel adventure, requiring everything we have all day long. Maintaining peak motivation is both crucial and a challenge made all the more difficult by blank rock. The art is to make the best of the situation; often the route is more interesting when an intricate way forward is found. We discover a no hands rest, eight meters below. From there, a shallow arch (we named Royal Arch) stretches left to the start of the Black Dihedral. It looks difficult, but if there is going to be a solution to our dilemma, it is Royal Arch and nothing else. We still feel defeated, turned back by a few meters of holdless granite that force us to weight one of the pegs in order to abseil down those eight meters to the no-hands rest. By evening, the pop of a beer can opening and a few honest gulps refresh our thoughts and prompt even wilder ones. Alexander suggests that instead of using the peg as an abseil anchor, we could use each other as living belay stations. The next morning, Alexander secures himself to the anchor with a meter of slack in the rope, and by sheer muscular strength, basically using his body as the anchor, and not weighting the belay bolts at all, holds the weight of my abseil to the no-hands rest. We have no idea if others will accept as valid this "manpowered rappel," but we are happy with it as an effective if unconventional solution to our free-climbing dilemma.

Our immediate goal is to draw closer to the Black Cave and, so we believe, the last significant obstacle barring the summit. Two fantastic corner pitches, followed by a short 5.12 face, and Alexander begins to unravel the geological mystery of the Black Cave. Right in the middle of the roof, in the wildest position imaginable, he finds an improbable no-hands rest. The last six meters to the normal belay point look extremely difficult and the only protection is a sawed-off angle, fixed in a groove at the lip of the roof. This pitiful peg will protect the crossover sequence above this wild abyss, where a dropped piton falls for over twenty seconds, never hitting the wall before impacting the ground. Some might be tempted to sink a bolt here, but this feels like a sacrilege for the most storied section of the North American Wall. Alexander makes several attempts at the crossover and every time ends up climbing back to sit by the sawed-off angle. He tries once more and this time he cracks it at 5.13b. There is no reversing things now. He swings his feet up onto the ledge and snatches the next hold. Now three meters past the sawn-off angle, the belay is only a short way above. He vanishes over the edge of the roof. The rope slowly pays out. All I can do is wait — wait for him to come flying over the roof, or wait for his cry of relief when he reaches the anchors. He screams. He's got the belay bolts. That son of a bitch has nerves of steel. Thirty-four years after Chuck Pratt had fought his way out "The most spectacular lead in American climbing," Alexander has turned the Black Cave pitch into free-climbing art.

We spend the next three days hopping route to route and discovering the only possible line through the steep upper wall. Four of the pitches are 5.12 or harder. On top at last we collapse, caked in sweat and dirt. It has taken fourteen climbing days to solve the massive puzzle of the Southeast Face. Much of the free line followed the NA Wall, but owing to hairline cracks, impossible to climb free, we often were forced to seek variations. The final free route combines parts of Continental Drift, New Jersey Turnpike, North America Wall, Sea of Dreams, and many new variations — all told, a fiercesome, 28-pitch medley with an identity all its own. We coin the route "El Nino."

The first ascent is over and our curiosity abated. But the project is only half done. Only when we both have red-pointed El Nino, during one continuous push, will the project be a legitimate climb and not merely an aerial boulder problem. After two days of rest, following drawn out breakfasts in the cafeteria and swimming in the Merced River, our batteries are once more fully charged. And off we go.

We both knock off the Black Dike and the Missing Link first try, but I stumble over the Galapagos. Alexander had already redpointd this pitch. As I follow, I switch feet and blow off a friction hold. Each redpoint burn requires enormous energy, so falls are disheartening. After a short break at the belay, I look up at the Galapagos again and have the same electrifying feeling I have when about to take the lead. This time the foot swap works and shortly the first crux section is behind us. On the second day, we climb without pause, all the way to the top of the Black Dihedral, anchor off our ropes and abseil down to our bivouac on Big Sur.

On the morning of day three, we climb the Black Cave straight off, then settle into a focused groove for the home stretch. We are so absorbed by the climbing and the excitement of completing the red point that we hardly notice dark clouds brewing in the distance. With 100 meters to go and all most all the major difficulties behind us, a light rain begins to fall. We crank up the speed. If the exit face gets too wet we will never climb it free, so the rush is on to avoid another night on the wall. We're climbing right at our limit now. Any faster would be dangerous. Our luck holds. The rain is still no more than a thin mist, and we top out a short while later.

Nearly 1,000 meters of incredible free-climbing lie beneath us. Our feet ache and our hands are shredded. Then the sky opens up and rain pours down. El Nino is blowing, bringing a change of climate. Climbing El Cap in the new millennium will be a brand new game, as wild and innovative as it was for the pioneers who first scaled the great wall forty years ago. We shoulder the haul bag and start for the East Ledges. Soon we are soaked to the bone. And we are ecstatic.

LURKING FEAR (2000)

Beth Rodden

From *The Valley Climbers*

2000, I walked up to Tommy Caldwell and invited him to try and free climb Lurking Fear, on El Capitan.

"Know anything about the route?" he asked. "Not a whole lot," I said. In fact I had no idea where Lurking Fear even started. Not that it mattered.

I was nineteen and up for anything.

Hanging in slings at the top of a grassy corner, I stare up at a grueling looking, 5.11 offwidth crack. That sick, empty feeling creeps back into my stomach. My arms feel like sandbags. It's the heat of the summer and we're going on a month working the route, day three on this push, and I barely have the strength to feed out slack and belay.

"How will I ever climb this pitch?" I wonder. I've found solace in the past four leads, none over 5.10, thinking the hard climbing is finally and thankfully over. Now this.

"Off belay, Beth!" yells Tommy from Thanksgiving Ledge, eighty feet above.

"Crap. This is not going to be fun," I grumble as I chalk

up and cram myself into the hateful off-size gash.

Lurking Fear lies on the western skyline of El Capitan. From the comfort of El Cap meadow, you can make out the first three pitches before the route snakes left around the corner. I had first heard mention of the climb a few years earlier, from my friend Brittany Griffith, who thought the whole route might go free. Back then I was a skinny little sport climber and a virgin to free-climbing El Cap granite. The Nose had schooled me several months earlier, but I had more gusto than I could harness and I needed something huge and extreme to absorb my enthusiasm.

In the spring of 2000, I walked up to Tommy Caldwell and invited him to join me for a free attempt on *Lurking Fear*. He'd recently lost his climbing partner to a family emergency, had just come off a free ascent of the Salathé Wall and was fluent in long hard free climbs.

"Know anything about the route?" he asked.

"Not a whole lot," I said. In fact I had no idea where Lurking Fear even started. Not that it mattered. I was nineteen and up for anything.

Tommy wondered out loud about my El Cap resume, which consisted of speed climbing champion Hans Florine and his wife dragging me up The Nose, a few months earlier. But I liked impossible goals, and sensed the same in Tommy. And with only three other free routes on El Cap, the idea of bagging a fourth was sure to win him over. I was super motivated to jump out of sport climbing and onto the big time. I needed this climb badly.

"It's getting kind of late in the season, but I've got

nothing going," Tommy finally said, smiling. I think he liked me.

"We can do it," I promised. "It'll be a riot." I sprang up and started racking gear because I couldn't wait. Of course I had no idea whatsoever about our chances, or what was involved. I only knew about my passion for Valley life: climbing till the sun went down, swimming in the river, and waking up so sore I could scream. I jumped at any chance to continue. Who wouldn't?

Several days later, when I muscled the huge pack onto my back, my legs quivered and I doubted I could hike the pig more than ten feet down the road without spraining something important. But I was dead set on impressing Tommy so I forged on anyway. Unbeknownst to me, friends were trying to hook us up, and to them, Lurking Fear was the perfect catalyst.

"Wow. That's one blank slab," I think as Tommy aids up the bolt ladder to string a top rope. A sea of grey, featureless granite soars above us for over 200 feet, with no knobs, ribs, or distinguishing features. Having grown up cragging in Smith Rock, Oregon, I'm no stranger to technical routes. However, pitch three of Lurking Fear redefines hard slab climbing.

Several hours later and bleeding from several fingertips, I slink onto the rope. My joints ache from crimping like mad and my skin is ripping through. But Tommy and I are in the beginning stages of our personal relationship, and I won't disappoint him. Or myself. Self-doubts are already eating me alive. "Was that all you had?" "Did you try every possible sequence?" "Can't your skin hack another try?" I suck it up and pull down. Salvation lies above.

I reach my left hand to a harsh sidepull, a quarter inch in size, and heave my weight over two time bomb footholds that threaten to crumble. Sharp pain shoots through my left index finger as I cross my right hand up to a nothing hold. I draw a deep breath and readjust my left hand as blood oozes from my fingertips.

"Watch me!" I yell down to Tommy, who's ready to nod. I've been up here so long.

I lean back, reel close into the wall and fling sideways, flying across the blank section between holds. My body arcs to a stop, feet scrabbling against the wall, hands down-pulling a positive hold.

"Amazing!" Tommy screams from below. "I didn't know you could dyno like that."

"Neither did I!" I shout back. Then I smile, set my feet, and climb to the anchors. Both of us are shocked that I pulled off this sideways dyno, which unlocks the sequence for the first crux section. The next day we both redpoint the pitch. We're on our way.

On a route with so much high-angled, razor-edged crimping, we had a limited number of burns to throw down before toes and calves started yelling out loud and finger pads blew out. We'd work crux sections, sometimes for days, and once our fingertips, energy and provisions ran out, we'd return to the ground, stringing fixed ropes behind. After a quick respite to let fingers heal up and to sleep fifteen hours a day, we'd return to the high point for another multi-day pull down.

Unlike sport routes, where the climbing moves are all that matter, working out a free route on the Captain involves hiking mammoth loads, jumaring and rappelling thousands of feet of fixed lines, hauling multiple pigs (haulbags), engineering and maintaining a hanging base of operations, and climbing your brains out. In the process, my "normal" life slowly naturalized to the vertical world. Everything ended up on the wall, and our bodies were the conduit to get it there. It took weeks to grow accustomed to the tremendous labor involved. Luckily, I was nineteen, so I recovered in a matter of hours. My sport climber legs turned into hiking machines, and jugging fixed lines became as natural as walking.

As my fitness increased, so did my appetite for climbing way off the deck, as well as my skill with logistics. Tommy was a terrific ropemate — patient, understanding and psyched. Most of all he showed me how to throw down my best effort and to block out everything else. Our partnership was working well.

By mid-May, daytime temperatures hovered in the high 80's — far from ideal for the thin climbing on Lurking Fear. So I'd crawl off our portaledge every morning before dawn and climb when the rock was shady and cool. After weeks of yanking on razor edges and cramming my feet into torturous, undersized shoes, my hands and feet were terribly swollen and my fingers looked like they'd been fed through a shredder. But we continued to make slow but steady progress, so never mind the pain. After many sorties spread over thirty days, with ropes fixed well up the wall, we geared up for the final push.

Three of the best splitter cracks in the Valley await us, a welcome contrast to the flesh-eating crux pitch we just finished. If any of these leads were on the Valley floor, lines at the base would stretch to Fresno. Windmilling up these soaring cracks, I finally feel like a climber in one of those quintessential El Cap pictures I grew up with — sun shining, hair blowing in the breeze, hands and feet jammed in the finest rock on earth.

I was raised in a climbing gym under the watchful eyes (a poster) of Lynn Hill, free-climbing The Nose. "It goes, boys!" was my common refrain. With her cut-off jean shorts, pink tank top and blonde hair, I wanted to be like Lynn. I've dreamed about free-climbing on El Cap, and many times have watched Lynn's video on free-climbing The Nose. Finally, after years of comps and clipping bolts, I've busted out for good. Thirty days of pain and effort have transformed me into the climber in the picture, hair blowing in the breeze, high on the ramparts of the Big Stone. I'm smiling out loud, knowing I am really, quintessentially here. My feet no longer hurt and my fingers feel fine. I unclip a cam off my rack, shove it into the crack and jam on. Slowly, we inch up the wall.

The last question mark pitch looms just above the splitters: A short, ominous traversing pitch that stymied Steve Schneider during the first, all out free attempt on the route in 1996. Hanging at the belay, gazing east across the gold rock, it looks much easier than pitch three. How wrong I am. Good edges and solid footholds lead to an encouraging crack where I can shake out before a few tenuous moves into the big blankness.

"Where did all the holds go?" I ask Tommy.

"You can do it," he encourages. But there are no dime-sized edges to clasp, no crumbling footholds to nurse into a sequence. One or two tiny flakes fleck the wall, facing the wrong way and not nearly good enough to support body weight. I hang on the rope and fondle the holds for what feels like hours. I must look like a mime up here, never quite unweighting the line, pretending to do a sequence over and over again. It's slowly registering that we're finished, that here is the impossible blank section we feared all along and that, finally, will do our dreams to death.

Weeks of brutal, painful work into all those crux pitches below, layers and layers of skin, a thousand hopes and for what? If I can't link the entire route, it means zero, nothing at all. The thought of failing poisons my soul. I inwardly writhe, once again cannibalized by vicious self-doubts — that I can't climb with the best of them, that I belong in a gym, not in Yosemite, that I'm just not good enough. The sun is not shining. My hair is not blowing in the breeze. The picture shows me rapping off. I am nothing.

I can barely speak to Tommy, or eat, or take a drink. I try and force myself asleep but all I can think about are those three pathetic holds. Why couldn't they face the right way? Why isn't there another foothold? There just isn't, that's why. I have to figure out a way for myself. I feel like screaming.

The next morning, Tommy ties in and starts climbing.

He gets spanked by the first few moves and can't solve the blankest puzzle we've ever seen. I watch intently, eyes glued to his feet and hands, hoping he unlocks the sequence. Grunting, but staying calm and steady on the short slab, he thrutches one hand above another. Climbing just out of sight now, I think he might have figured out the sequence, but no celebratory screams follow. "Crap," I mumble. "How the hell are we going to do this?"

"Off belay!" He yells. It takes a moment to set in. He never said "Take." He never weighted the rope.

"Did you send it?" I shout back.

"Yes!" He yells, then pauses. "But there's no way you can do it that way. I was totally stretched out." Then another pause. I can tell he is torn. Should he celebrate cranking final crux pitch, or sympathize with me and my doubtful task ahead? That's Tommy Caldwell, kind to a fault. "No worries. I'll give it another shot," I yell, feigning confidence.

A wave of drive swells in me. I used to feel this force field when I competed, right before latching the starting holds. My limbs hum with energy. I won't let a measly ten feet of slab climbing keep me from impressing Tommy and proving that I belong on El Capitan. I will not retire with nothing at all. I lace up my shoes, dip in for a final chalk, and crank on.

I had hoped and half expected to ride that force field to the belay, but my arms feel shot and my legs are shaky. For several days I've woken up to seizing muscles. I'm only a sport climber who's surpassed her limits fifty times, and ten times too many. But I will pound my head against this wall until I am physically done, entirely used up, before I quit and crawl off to the cafeteria.

I punch a hand into a good crack and jam upwards over smooth granite. Just above, Tommy hangs at the anchors, smiling slightly, but with worried eyes. He knows how desperately I need this. But he cannot help me now.

I exit the crack and move up on small edges. My fingers, though terribly sore, are used to the continual crimping. After a few moves I arrive at the dreaded three holds. If I grab them harder, stand harder on my footholds as well, and simply don't let go, then just maybe I can make this. One hold after another, I slowly move upwards. My legs start shaking. "Crap," I think, "Relax. You're going to fumble it." Then I spot a smear I'd never seen before. Relief, anticipation, and ten different thoughts shoot through me. "That's amazing?" "Why didn't I see this before!?" "You better not blow this!" "Stop thinking!" I shout internally. "The smear means nothing if you don't buck up and do it."

I paste my right foot on the merest bump. My foot stays for a second, then my toes start to creep and panic sets in.

"Come on, Rodden!" I yell in my mind. "Dig deep. Deeper than ever."

At maximum crimp, I push on my foot and tell myself I have super glue on it. The foot continues creeping. I slowly press my leg straight, balancing against the golden granite.

"Oh my God," I think excitedly, "This is it!" Then fear

snaps: "Don't fuck up!" My left hand reaches a positive Gaston which I clench hard, as if to save my life. It provides slight stability until my right hand can snatch a good edge.

"Holy crap, you just did it!" I rave to myself. I can't believe it. The weeks of hard work. I pause, not moving, clutching what feel like the two best holds in the world. My heart hammers like a drum. I slowly come back to earth, 700 meters up El Cap, and realize there still are hard moves ahead, so I calm myself and carefully climb to the anchor. There's more to come, for sure, but the crux is behind us now.

With several more efforts spread over the following two weeks, we thrutch and muscle and finesse our way up through the last of the hard climbing. Toward the end of the final week, a withering, whole body fatigue starts in my core and creeps out to my fingers and toes. Burning and exhausted, I barely reach the top of each pitch.

At the end of "The Grand Traverse," we planned to rest a day and then push for the summit. But my anticipation is so great I can't stand it and press Tommy to gun for the top.

"We can do it," I gleam. "It's pretty easy climbing. Just one 5.11 pitch, then the top. The top!"

"If you're up for it," Tommy smiles, and off we go, pulling for the clouds.

Lurking Fear was the start of it all for me and Tommy. We spent much of the next decade, including our honeymoon, on the side of El Capitan. I learned that, like the steepest route in the world, marriage is a long and varied puzzle. Sometimes all the holds are there and sometimes not. And in the end, there weren't enough holds for us and we fell apart. When it first set in that I had failed, that I had lost my best friend, husband and climbing partner, my self-doubts tore me down harder than El Cap ever could. I questioned life, and every choice I ever made. But slowly, I started to see another line, one where brute force and will power found no purchase. So on a high wire of patience, acceptance, and forgiveness, I made a few moves forward. Yet I wondered: What if I can't go big without Tommy? What if he was the spark who ignited my drive and passion?

After a stay at my parents I returned to Yosemite Valley. Since our divorce, I associate too much of El Cap with Tommy, and until now it has been a mountain to overcome. So I've mostly bouldered, sometimes feeling like a lost girl, ranging around the Valley floor and wondering what comes next. But this time I drove straight to El Cap Meadow. Gazing up at my old friend, I took a deep breath and closed my eyes as memories burst from the middle of me — the laughing, the crying, being scared out of my mind, and climbing harder than I ever thought possible. I have lost so many things, and my longing was measured in tears. I miss the wind, the smell in the mornings, the sparrows shooting by at high speeds, and holding a hand offered me. I miss the hard, honest labor that goes with climbing the wall, the dedication and drive it takes to summit. I am due for shoulder surgery this winter, but in the spring and summer of recovery, the Captain will be with me.

EL CORAZÓN! (2001)

Alexander Huber

From *The Valley Climbers*

Up here there are no guarantees. The pitches are long and exhausting, the exposure outrageous and the protection is rarely ideal.

Max Reichel and I are 1,500 feet up El Capitan, bivouacked on a ledge in the shadow of the Nose. It is the dead of night. I lie in my sleeping bag, bolt awake. The overhanging cliff soars above. The moon must have risen over Half Dome, around the corner and five miles east. Far below, Yosemite Valley is washed in pale white light.

El Corazón is my fifth free climbing route on the Captain. I've climbed dozens of other big walls, from the granite towers of the Karakoram to the ice plastered needles of Patagonia. And yet at the start of every free ascent I still get nervous. Up here there are no guarantees. The pitches are long and exhausting, the exposure outrageous and the protection is rarely ideal. Long falls are expected. Every route has the aspect of a thriller because I can never know the ending beforehand. From the first move till the last step onto the summit I'm strung tight between hope and fear. All this adrenaline robs my sleep, but I cannot live without it.

Free climbing Yosemite big walls began as an adventurous sideshow to the sport climbing movement that dominated climbing from the early 1980s. In 1993, Lynn Hill became first to free climb every pitch of an El Cap route with her historic free ascent of the Nose. Two years later I made the first redpoint ascent of the mythic Salathe Wall. These were isolated ascents, however, as long before, top free climbers had left the Valley for Smith Rocks, American Forks, Verdon, Buoux, and beyond.

Like the tide coming home once more, attention shifted back to Yosemite in 1998, when my brother Thomas and I free climbed an intricate variation of North America Wall we named El Niño. El Cap was quickly reassessed in light of modern sport climbing standards, and what people saw was a limitless frontier of splitter cracks, wild corners, and giant roofs — many lifetimes of futuristic free climbs awaiting exploration. Young British climbers Leo Houlding and Patch

Hammond, Austrian Much Mayr, Japanese champion Yuji Hirayama, and of course the remarkable Tommy Caldwell, often partnered by Beth Rodden, soon lit El Cap on fire with historic free ascents. Since the turn of the century, free ascents of Yosemite big walls have increased dramatically, as climbers from many lands embrace this high stakes game of experience, courage, muscle, and adrenaline.

Adrenalin! I am awake with first light. As day slowly streams into the Valley I lay in my bag, staring straight up. The faint shadow line of Beak Flake runs eighty meters down the otherwise featureless wall — and ends ten meters above my head. Between the flake and this ledge looms a wave of smooth granite: the crux of El Corazón. My only protection is a Bird Beak, a tiny, hook-bladed piton set in a shallow seam eight meters above. A fall might snap the slender metal beak or rip it from the seam, dashing me onto the ledge. I can only risk such a fall if I know I can flash the body length of moves between the sketchy Bird Beak and the start of Beak Fake. But like every free climbing venture on the big stone, I'm on a voyage into the unknown. Calculating risks and managing danger will determine success — or shattered legs.

I tie into the rope and a very attentive Max starts to belay. Yet I feel like I am free soloing. I am scared, but stuff the fear before it explodes into terror. Slowly, I move upwards, passing the Bird Beak and finally reaching two sidepulls. I jack my feet high onto footholds till I am fully coiled. Then I draw a quick breath — and jump. Both arms windmill up as my torso arches, skimming the rock. My sights are fixed, my timing true and my fingers latch the start of Beak Flake. I set my feet and briefly glance down at the short face, barely 10 meters of a 900 meter wall, but featuring everything I associate with free climbing El Capitan: athleticism, guts, imagination, precision, and most of all, heart: El Corazón!

FREE RIDER IN A DAY (2004)

Steph Davis

From *The Valley Climbers*

I closed my eyes for a second and slumped against the wall until Heinz scolded me to keep going. Times like these, when it's just all fatigue, are a part of every El Cap experience.

We walked to the base slowly, in the early evening. We had decided that I should start at 6:00 p.m., giving me daylight for the insecure 5.11 slabs on the Free Blast, the initial thousand feet up the Salathé Wall. If I climbed fast, I could gain Heart Ledge by dark and then start climbing by headlamp. I was hoping to gain the little rest niche at the Alcove, about halfway up the wall, by 6:00 am. However Heinz insisted we would be there by 2:00 a.m. at the latest, and he put two superlight down sleeping bags in the pack so we could steal a few hours of sleep before dawn.

We were a little early at the base, and as I organized my gear a young black bear silently approached. Heinz and I looked at him in delight. "A good sign!" we told each other, laughing, as he ambled off to the west.

At 5:45, I could wait no longer. I gave Heinz a big hug and set off, full of excitement and anxiety. We had one rope; there was no going down. Working the slabby crux pitches high on the Free Blast, it felt like I was barely moving. I was shocked when Heinz told me that it had been only two hours since we left the ground.

As I finished the downclimb to Heart Ledge, I switched on my headlamps. Two Austrians were lying there in sleeping bags, a little surprised to see me. In full blackness, I started the next lead, pitch twelve, enjoying climbing within my little circle of light. I carefully navigated up, across, and down, and started chugging up the flared chimney of Hollow Flake. In the absence of any protection, my rope snaked down into the darkness, making this essentially a free solo. My nervousness was replaced by the calm that comes from a big climbing push. Just keep on keeping on . . .

I first started working Free Rider (VI 5.12d, 38 pitches) in the fall of 2004. Pioneered by German climbers Alex and Thomas Huber in 1998, Free Rider follows the Salathé Wall, on the Southwest Face of El Capitan, except for a four pitch variation around the Salathé's 5.13 headwall. After several attempts spread over three months, I was starting to make good progress, but had to leave the Valley after getting stormed off the wall on Halloween night. I returned at the end of March, fired up to redpoint the route. On April 24, I topped out after four days on the wall, having made the first female free ascent, and led

163

every pitch.

Two weeks later my friend Heinz Zak arrived from Austria to shoot photos of me. I climbed the crux leads of Free Rider once again, and as we camped on top that night, Heinz said, "You looked great on those pitches. You should do it in a day." A one-day free ascent of El Capitan is one of free climbing's greatest prizes. The idea had crossed my mind as something to try later, maybe next season. But Heinz meant now — like right now, after a few rest days. And he offered to come along for support, carrying the pack, belaying, and following every pitch. How could I turn down such an offer?

Way up in the blackness, I groveled up the hideous Monster Off width Crack below the Alcove, roughly 1,600 feet up the Captain. The darkness hid the wild exposure, and I was surprised to feel totally relaxed, climbing much faster and more efficiently than I had imagined. Heinz was right, and we reached the Alcove around 2:00 a.m. I peeled off my climbing shoes, pulled on a pair of socks and dozed until I woke shaking with cold at 5:30 a.m.

It was hard to get going, and I was thankful I'd brought a little plastic bottle of espresso — icy cold, but effective. I tried to ignore the headache I'd had since starting the climb twelve hours before. How could I have forgotten aspirin? Probably just nerves, because I had no idea what was going to happen on the notorious Huber Pitch, the crux of the route looming not far overhead.

During my initial attempts on Free Rider, the Huber Pitch had stumped me completely. Toward the end of the pitch I had to climb into a tenuous stance, my fingers clinging in opposite directions on a wrinkle in front of my face — as though trying to pry open an elevator door — and then explode into an all-out sideways leap to a slanting hold. If I did manage to catch it, I'd need to hang on with both hands as my body flew sideways, like a cat in a hurricane latched onto a flagpole. Two thousand feet up El Cap. With a single spinning buttonhead bolt for gear between me and my belayer. The move seemed completely improbable. But I realized that the body positions for setting up to leap were similar to certain yoga poses, so back home in Moab, Utah, I did warrior poses day after day. I also realized that only two or three moves were stopping me — basically a body length of granite in over 3,000 feet of climbing. Uncharacteristically that winter, I never tied in to a rope, choosing to boulder at Big Bend and climb on my backyard wall in order to increase my power for those moves.

The following spring I once more found myself at the belay beneath the Huber Pitch. The weather was cold and stormy. I was shaking and my feet were numb. I took off my shoes and blew into them, tried to steel myself, and started to climb. I felt strong as I cranked into the warrior stance. I tried not to wonder if the old buttonhead bolt would hold a fall, and as I jumped left my belayer gave me lots of slack. I hit the hold, but too low to stick it, feeling helpless as I flew downward, banging sideways along the slab below. I lowered off, untied, and pulled the rope. I couldn't stop shaking.

I put on a jacket and looked up at the rock. I started the moves again, feeling weaker, but absolutely committed.

When I got to the warrior stance, I leaped with everything I had. This time I latched the hold with both hands. As my body flew left, I kicked my feet against the wall and made the next long pull into the layback crack. Still quivering, I kept my concentration until I reached the belay and then started yelping with delight. I felt stunned, like I'd just exploded through an actual wall to another place and was looking around, shaking off bits of drywall.

A little before six in the morning, I gathered my energy, dove into the dripping, slippery Jungle Pitch, and soon we were at the Block. Heinz started talking about the summit, still several cruxes away. Always a bad idea.

Scrapping up flaring, funky jams and laybacks, the first hard dihedral pitch felt shockingly easy. "5.9 for you!" shouted Heinz cheerfully. The next one was not as smooth. As I writhed up the slopy, funky corner, I started scrapping above frayed pieces of sling material, cinched onto broken, knotted bashie cables — and somehow managed to fight to a stance. I'd spent far too much energy, and as I reached the end of the pitch, I felt myself falling out of a flared hand jam — but kept pulling and somehow landed my other hand in just as I started to pitch. At the belay I felt cold, exhausted, and mad at my inelegant performance. Irrationally, I expected to fall and somehow die on the next traverse pitch. The lack of sleep was getting to me.

The traverse wraps left, around the side of the Salathé Wall, and the rope grates across grainy aretes. It is unbelievably exposed, with long, powerful, insecure moves on big sloping holds — the final crux of the route.

I made the big moves around the first arete, feeling like I might fall off every hold. This 5.12 pitch ends with a frightening off-balance undercling sequence, the last piece of gear out of sight around a gritty corner. I feared that if I whipped off, the rope would shred on the rough arete and I would keep going straight down, plunging thousands of feet to the Valley floor — good incentive not to fall. I was in a daze as I powered through the undercling and climbed up to Round Table Ledge. I was grumpy and tired and didn't feel like climbing the final three steep pitches to the top. I closed my eyes for a second and slumped against the wall until Heinz scolded me to keep going. Times like these, when it's just all fatigue, are a part of every El Cap experience.

I started reorganizing the rack, finally got it together as soon as my hands sank into the next dihedral, I suddenly felt a flow of energy. Steep cracks! My favorite! I started running up the corner, laughing and feeling punchy. It had been about twenty hours since we left the ground, but everything was fun again.

We reached the top in the afternoon sun and Heinz checked his watch: 4:00 p.m. on May 24, exactly one month since the last time I had topped out. As I sprawled on the warm granite slab, I looked at Heinz, overwhelmed with gratitude. He really had given this day to me — one of the best climbs of my life. Suffused with the contentment of exhaustion, I was not the same person who had stood at the foot of El Cap one long day before.

THE DIHEDRAL WALL (2004)

Tommy Caldwell

From *The Valley Climbers*

I would start at 5:00 a.m., climb from the ground to the end of the last hard pitch 1,800 feet up the wall, rappel back to the ground by noon, eat lunch, then boulder till dark. My fingers were bloody stumps and my toenails fell off.

"I don't know if I have this in me anymore."

My very words scare the shit out of me because I have never backed off no matter what. I will press on and I will prove I am capable. But 1,800 feet up El Cap, I've pumped out once again after more than an hour on a red point burn. With each fall, and each time savagely reclimbing the pitches, the Captain has claimed a little more of me. Now, after throwing myself at this wall for over sixty days, my arms seize when I raise them and blood seeps from holes in my fingers, knees, elbows, shins, and forehead. One short pitch from sure success, and I'm on the verge of shutdown.

The Dihedral Wall is perhaps the most natural appearing line on El Capitan, and was the third route climbed, after the Nose (1958) and the Salathé (1961). Back then (1962), the Dihedral was a traditional "nail-up" from bottom to top. Alan Lester and Pete Takeda free climbed half the route in the early 1990s. Then Todd Skinner and Paul Piana worked the line extensively in 2001 and 2002, pioneering the variations I would follow for my all out, free attempt. When I aid-soloed the Dihedral in October 2003, the climb looked unimaginably hard as a free route. Steep, slanting corners shot upwards for hundreds of feet — thin throughout the bottom half, flared and bottoming up high. Sometimes the cracks melded into smooth granite. I'd have to put in months of extreme effort, if not several seasons worth, to know if I had a real shot at freeing the route.

I came to Yosemite early that spring — alone, since Beth Rodden, my wife and usual El Cap partner back then, was recovering from a stress fracture in her foot. The weather was crisp and clear, perfect for a good old El Cap beat down. After months of sport climbing, I needed an adventure, something huge to demolish my body and my days, with the curse of failure to drive me.

At first I worked the route solo, toproping on my fixed lines. Alone, I could focus entirely on the beauty and magnitude of the climb. Slowly I grew accustomed to the silence, to my inner voice insisting I crank harder. Every leaning corner, fingertip edge and hairline fracture — and the thousands of moves I rehearsed — was etched into memory. No other El Cap free route had so many difficult pitches stacked one on top of the other. Some leads were so continuous I felt shattered after half a rope length. I wanted this one real bad, so the more I hurt, the deeper I dug. I loved this shit. When a toe would skid or my fingers buttered off I'd scream. Then I might hang still and silent, watching swallows tackle each other in midair and then plummet, separating and flaring just before the treetops. Alone on the dark wall I lived for no one but myself. Few might understand, but so it goes.

I climbed four or five days a week from sunrise to sunset. On my biggest days I would start at 5:00 a.m., climb from the ground to the end of the last hard pitch 1,800 feet up the wall, rappel back to the ground by noon, eat lunch, then boulder till dark. My fingers were bloody stumps and my toenails fell off. My muscles were so sore I forgot what normal felt like. I would call Beth at night and fall asleep on the phone.

Trips home mainly consisted of sleep and food. "What's wrong with you?" Beth would ask, but deep inside she knew. I'd come to thrive on pain, as the Dihedral Wall consumed me. But nothing compared to how I loved Beth. That is why, when things unraveled between us eight years later, it almost killed me. I gave everything to her. In the end, she took it and ran. It felt like a leader fall that would never end, us plummeting for the treetops, then watching her flare off in a direction all her own. I should never know why, exactly.

I returned to the Valley and once more hurled myself at El Capitan. At the end of each day I would stagger to my car and try to patch my wounds. I'd shove food down my throat as quickly as possible, usually cold burritos, or sometimes just a PowerBar. I would find a place to sleep and pass out soon as my head hit the pillow. Occasionally I fell asleep sitting straight up while cooking dinner, only to be rousted by the rangers telling me to move on. I felt like an addict, climbing myself to a coma, driven by forces I was unable or unwilling to stop. If only I could increase my threshold for pain and struggle, my thinking ran, push it beyond what anyone else could manage, then maybe the Dihedral Wall could be mine.

After another month, I could link long sections, then entire pitches. Soon I had toproped most of the hard climbing. Originally I considered this a recon season, logging endless laps to get the pitches dialed. Now, with perfect weather and demonic drive, I was cramming several seasons of climbing into a couple of months. It looked like obsession to friends and family, but it was far worse. The spectacular beauty and unlikelihood of the project were half its allure, but I was chasing a treacherous flame. Of course the climb had completely taken me over, and as the fire raged, I gave into it and let it consume me, rather than seeking help.

Beth finally got her foot out of the cast, and she was now at her parents' house in Davis, only a three-hour drive from the Valley. When I told her I thought I could send the route, she offered to come along as belayer. Adam Stack, fresh off a free ascent of the Salathé, also volunteered to help out. I would have been completely astonished by their generosity if I hadn't seen it so many times before.

Three days before casting off, Adam and I hauled five

days' worth of supplies to the top of pitch nine. This would allow us to climb without hauling for the first two days. As everything fell into place my heart rate increased and I spent nights tossing and turning, endlessly rehearsing the climb in my head. When should I start? How fast do I need to climb? How many times can I fall before running out of energy? I visualized the moves and gear placements over and over: blue, then purple, then baby yellow. That fire was burning me to ashes. I needed to send. Bad! With so much invested, I was terrified of failure.

I had to go home with the prize.

We begin climbing at 5:00 a.m. on May 18, 2003. The weather is unseasonably cool, perfect for free-climbing. I flash the first four pitches in 90 minutes; Beth says she is jumaring slower than I am climbing 5.12. On the fifth pitch I forget half the rack and have to throw down a 25-foot run out on 5.12. I take it in stride and pull up to the crux pitch by eight am. Just above, shooting through a 120-foot bulge, the route exits the lower, left-facing dihedrals and climbs out right onto the steep wall near Cosmos. It seems as though here, a rampart of the French sport climbing area, Ceüse, was grafted onto El Cap. When working the route I never completely linked this pitch on toprope, but hoped the psyche of the redpoint attempt might carry me through. This would likely be the hardest free pitch on the Captain. I'd have to modulate my breathing, hit the sequence perfectly and most of all, to try like hell to ever get the send. I give Beth a kiss and set off.

I start laybacking up a one-foot-wide dihedral with no

crack in the back, pressing my feet hard against the wall, testing my shoe rubber to the limit. Then the crack ends and I make a full span right to a sloping ramp, then dyno for a shallow finger lock. Pumped now, my body shakes horribly from the strain. I can't hear Beth and Adam's screams of encouragement, which leave them hoarse. Already redlining, I press my thumbs up underneath a small roof and stretch to an undercling far above my head. As I pull into the undercling I nearly faint from dizziness. I desperately fumble for high crimpers, then pull over into a "5.13 stance" on the slab above. My legs shake uncontrollably and my mind races. "Ten more feet and it's over," I tell myself.

I focus, try to compose myself, then delicately traverse on micro holds to the stance at the belay. I clip the bolted anchor and scream between gasping breaths. Beth and Adam jumar up and we erect the portaledge so I can lie down and regroup. The next pitch is 5.13b, slabby and sharp, and it is crucial to get it the first try to save skin for the rest of the route. I balance from razor to razor. The slightest shake and I'll rip. Beth and Adam are silent. After nearly an hour I arrive at the anchor. Half the day's climbing is below me and it is only ten in the morning. I'm encouraged, but I will not be so fresh in the afternoon, or in the days to come.

The next pitch follows the Black Arch, a 200 foot arcing crack and one of the most striking features on El Cap. The sun strikes the wall just as I start up. I feel uncertain, and slip off after 20 feet — my first fall of the route. I rest ten minutes, pull my rope, and try again, pumping out after

30 feet. Adam sets up the portaledge and I rest for half an hour. Next try I pump out after 35 feet. I start to worry that I might be through, that I don't have it in me.

I rest for about 40 minutes, pull the rope again, and go for it once more, desperately managing to climb to the first rest, 40 feet up. My confidence is shot. For the next hour and a half, Beth and Adam blast me with encouragement. "Try hard Tommy, you can do it!" they yell. In my head, I rage at myself: "Don't be such a pansy. Just suck it up and climb!" I slowly creep up the arch, resting for long periods whenever possible. I feel like a sloth moving up the wall. Just as Beth and Adam are about to fall asleep I reach the anchor. I only have one more pitch before the cush bivy ledge with all of our stuff, but it's the second-hardest pitch of the climb. My toes are throbbing and blood spews from three of my fingernails. I need to bear down, tap into the blaze, and send.

I pull out of the Black Arch via underclings and sidepulls separated by gaps I can barely connect with the span of my arms. The pitch is the only slab I have ever climbed that maxes both my finger strength and arm power. I wrestle from feature to feature, shoving the pain off the edge of my mind, and finally arrive at the hardest single move of the climb — a six foot gap, blank except for a single shallow divot. Glad for the countless hours I've spent bouldering in the Valley, I grit my teeth, pull massively, and stretch for the divot. Matching one finger at a time in the divot and hopping my feet to higher smears, I start to fade. Panicked, I slap for a sloper above. My feet sketch off as I match hands and frantically smear my feet higher, sag on my arms and dyno with my last ounce of energy. My fingertips tag the edge of the jug above — and I'm off, tumbling down the wall like a pinball, wrenching to a stop 30 feet below.

I have no more energy. I pull on gear through the crux and climb to the ledge sixty feet above. Beth and Adam soon follow and set up camp. I pull off my shoes and lay back on the ledge, my pulse throbbing in my fingertips and toes. Never have I cranked so much difficult climbing in so short a time, and I fear I've overdone it. I can only lay there, my chest heaving and my body vibrating with pain. I have serious doubts about tomorrow. Beth gives me a massage and Adam talks about riding grizzly bears in Alaska. By the time the sun goes down I'm feeling rejuvenated. Adam and I rap down and I give the pitch another burn, but fall at the same place as my first go. I gave it one last try before dark, and fell at a lower point. We've been up since three in the morning and now it's nine at night and I still want more daylight. Beth is wasted — eight months off, then straight onto El Cap — but she still manages to give me a massage to help me sleep.

The next morning I feel sore but confident. I wolf down some canned peaches and beef jerky and lower 100 feet to warm up. The first few moves feel horrible, but after about ten minutes my fingers and toes numb a bit and I'm good to go.

Adam and I rap down to try pitch nine once again. I power quickly through the bottom and heave past the divot without error. I match on the sloper, get my feet up — and then do something that goes against everything

I know about climbing hard: I hesitate. Beth and Adam simultaneously yell, "Come on Tommy!" I sag back and dyno. This time my fingertips nab the hold. I let out a whoop and scramble onto the bivy ledge.

Above lay a 5.13c flaring hand and fist crack in a corner, a 5.13b rounded layback, and a wet, 5.12d offwidth. Any one of these pitches would form the crux of most any other free climb on El Cap, but here on the Dihedral they feel almost insignificant. I fall once on each pitch but muster the strength to climb each lead second try. By the end of the day my toes feel like they might pop through my climbing shoes. From head to toe, all I can feel is pain. It will ruin me, but I'll need to harness the intense, fiery waves of this pain in order to carry on. And I will carry on. Much of the hard climbing is below me now. Sitting there high on El Capitan, entranced by my heartbeat slamming through my arms and fingers, up through my back and neck, down my legs and into my toes, I'm starting to believe I have a chance to send this monster.

That night Adam heads back to the ground to teach a clinic. It feels weird to say goodbye in the middle of a wall. "Don't think that you're coming down, too," says Adam. "You run out of supplies, I'm jugging back up with more." We send Adam down with a walkie-talkie so he can humor us from 1,500 feet below. I hate to see him go, but I still have Beth, who has been a part of every free route I have done on the big stone, excepting my first time on the Salathé.

That night I lay awake listening to the sounds of the

waterfalls and trying to ignore my throbbing fingers and toes. I watched the "half sky" view of the stars and drop deeply into the calm embers of El Cap. Only three hard pitches remain: a soaking wet flare that because of pure nastiness I have barely worked; a horrendous boulder problem pitch; then another 5.13c that is the scariest lead of the climb. Bolt awake, I try not to toss and turn in the portaledge, so Beth can get a good night's sleep.

Next morning I crawl out of my sleeping bag with my eyes glued shut. By the time I gear up I'm bleeding from my fingers and knees. I stare at the pitch above, an arching black crack dripping with mud. My hands and feet are on fire, that throbbing is once more exploding through my body and climbing at all is terrible labor. My energy, my commitment, my desire is burned up and I have nothing on which to ride out this route but that fiery tide of pain. I focus on the next belay, struggle through the wet pitch and collapse on a precarious ledge. Ideally I wanted to link this mud section into the next pitch, producing another multi-crux, 5.13 beast; but if I fell on the boulder problem above, I couldn't bear the thought — and might not be able to — re-climb the soggy corner. I lay on the ledge for a half hour, in a trance, visualizing the upcoming moves. Then I commit and crank through the V9 boulder problem. Nearing the final jug, my feet swung wildly and I plunge off. I lower back to the ledge, pull the rope, and send the pitch next try.

Now everything is bleeding, oozing, smoldering. My core is clenched, my face fixed in a grimace. I'm demolished. My mind races. What now? Even my pain has burned itself out. There's just the one hard pitch left, but I can barely lift my head and my arms won't work. Could I rally later that afternoon? Tomorrow? It seems unlikely. This ruinous fatigue started consuming me from the inside months before. Hour by hour it can only get worse. I can barely arrange the belay.

I slump back, intent to pass out till evening when Adam's voice cracks over the radio. "Nice job dude!" he shouts. "I got a whole crowd of people down here waiting to see you send the last hard pitch." The solitary nature of big-wall free-climbing is to me its biggest draw. But this time, much as one absorbs the group energy while cragging, I focus on the crowd 2,800 feet below, and plumb just enough power to make a move. Then another. My body quivers with anguish and fatigue but I kept moving, fearing that if I stop I might freeze solid, or dry up and blow away. After concentrating for three days straight, my mind is as fried as my body. "It is almost over," I keep repeating. "It's almost over."

I move from a shallow groove to a small layback crack and the last ten feet of hard climbing. My teeth grind out loud as I start pulling. If I fall, a fixed pin, at least twenty years old and driven straight into mud, will hopefully catch me. I force my bloody, swollen fingertips against a tiny sidepull and smear my toes on a glassy dish. Just as my fingertips reach the next hold, my foot slips and I desperately re-smear my shoe and shoot my hand into a bomber jam above. The remaining 30 feet are the most carefully climbed 5.11 I have ever done. I pull over the top in shambles.

LOSING MYSELF ON HALF DOME (2008)

Alex Honnold

From *The Valley Climbers*

I had to do something soon; treading water was only wearing me out. I never considered downclimbing. I was going up — it was just a matter of how high — one way or another.

The idea of free soloing Half Dome had dominated my thoughts for the whole summer. An injury had forced me to take the season off from climbing, and I spent several months hiking around the Sierra. Mile after mile, week after week, Half Dome was my muse and source of motivation. By September I was back in shape, back in the Valley, and super psyched to resume hard climbing.

Half Dome is a beautiful face, intimidating yet alluring. I love the way it dominates the east end of the Valley. But why I had to solo the wall, I don't exactly know. Maybe I'd spent so much time imagining a solo ascent that nothing else could clear it from my mind. Perhaps no answer will ever do. For whatever reason, I decided that I would solo Half Dome.

I had free climbed the route once before, following a line too sketchy to try without a rope. Variations exist on most hard sections, so to determine the route best suited for free soloing, I repeated the climb with a partner. The reconnaissance went well and I managed the route without falls. I felt physically ready for the free solo.

The whole next day I spent sitting alone in my van, thinking about the route. Ideally, I would have climbed the wall a few more times to get the crux bits safely dialed. But each practice run required a full day and a willing partner. What's more, I had commitments for most of the coming months, and felt a little pressure to finish my solo projects before my partners arrived. This all left me conflicted about going up on Half Dome by myself. But ultimately, I decided to go for the solo the following day. I could hike back down if things felt wrong, though once I reached the cliff I knew I would never bail.

On a clear but blazing September morning, I began trudging up the half-mile of slabs beneath Half Dome. With every step I felt the great face looming over me. I kept my eyes down, and for the first time in months, tried not to think about the climb. My load was light so I moved quickly, but I was sweating like a dog by the time I finished the two hour approach.

Resting at the base I felt completely detached from the rest of the Valley landscape, glowing in the morning sun, another world below me. The whole Northwest Face towered in deep shade and I could see that for today, I had the wall entirely to myself. For the next few hours I would be alone in a unique way, locked in a high stakes game of solitude.

I slipped several energy bars in the pocket of my shorts, along with a plastic flask with a third liter of water. Finally there was nothing else to do but climb. I started up the first pitch — fun 10c pin scars, and a good warm up for the 2,000 feet of granite soaring overhead.

The initial leads passed quickly and I found myself below the "Higbee 'Hedral," a free variation that bypasses a bolt ladder on the original aid line. The 'Hedral makes for secure soloing since you could jump off the difficult, opening sequence and land on a big ledge. But these are amongst the route's hardest moves, and I had to shift from cruising up fun cracks to cranking on small holds. I laced my shoes extra tight and powered through the six-move boulder problem.

The rest of the pitch is filthy; trying to avoid dirt and bushes, I tracked the faint trail of chalk we'd laid down several days before. The moment I rejoined the normal route, I relaxed and shifted back into cruise mode. I had 1,000 feet of climbing till the next critical section, and I wanted to go slow and steady to preserve strength.

At mid-height, the route traverses right to a 50-foot bolt ladder leading to an enormous chimney system. On my previous free ascents, I bypassed the bolt ladder via a relatively new, 12c sport pitch. But as I climbed near I got spooked about soloing a dicey sequence up glossy slopers and scoops, followed by a down mantle on a crimp rail. I knew the original free variation (pioneered three decades before the 12c sport pitch) broke off a lead before, and circled around the whole section of wall, rejoining the route another rope length above. I'd never climbed this variation, but heard it was loose and dirty; but just then, adventurous 5.10 seemed more attractive than insecure 5.12+.

I broke off the normal route at a random point, and began wandering upward on flaky, open face climbing, searching for the 5.10 variation. After 50 feet I suddenly found myself in the middle of Half Dome, 1,000 feet off the deck, quite possibly off route, pulling past dirt and bushes. I was starting to get concerned.

Eventually I found some old slings, and directly below, a 100-foot 5.10 finger crack I had to slowly downclimb into the chimney system. The crack was distressingly thin for my fat fingers, and I felt immense relief to finally regain the clean, well-traveled corner. Moving slow and steady now, I regained my pace and confidence, ratcheting up the chimney for hundreds of feet.

At last I reached Big Sandy, an enormous ledge system 1,600 feet up the wall. I kicked back and unlaced my shoes. I had been climbing for over two hours and needed a breather. I finished off my small stash of food and water so I'd have nothing weighing me down for the remaining hard leads off the ledge. Finally, I relaced my shoes, set my iPod to repeat on some Eminem songs, and started climbing.

Just above, for three spectacular pitches, the notorious Zig-Zags follow a thin crack set in a steep, polished corner. Though the hardest section is rated 5.11d, with my fat fingers, it's always felt like 5.12. Aesthetically, the Zig-Zags represent the best Yosemite has to offer —

perfect corner cracks with staggering exposure. But I wasn't thinking about big air as I carefully cranked up the first pitch of tenuous, fingertip laybacking.

I climbed almost in a daze, moving on instinct, trying not to think about the extreme sections above, or the holdless, 5.11+ slab a pitch beyond the Zig-Zags. I moved steadily, one thin fingerlock at a time, up the steep dihedral. I pulled very hard. Every hold felt crisp and perfect.

The second Zig-Zag flew past in a flurry of hand jams and hero laybacking. With every zag in the crack, I'd punch out a roof on bomber hand jams, the Valley floor yawning 4,000 feet below. The pitch was a delight compared to the ferocious thin laybacks above and below. I paused at a stance beneath the third Zig-Zag, to make sure I don't get ahead of myself.

I was perhaps 1,700 feet up a vertical granite wall, balancing on a square of rock barely larger than my shoes. I could hear them now: "If your foot pops, you die," or "If you get stung by a bee, you'll die." But I've blown feet, had birds fly out of cracks, had bats hiss (which always scares the shit out of me), and nothing ever came out of it. I remembered this when, after a two minute breather, I pulled into a vertical corner, once more heaving off flared, fingertip jams with both feet pasted flush on a smooth granite wall. I knew exactly what to do, and quickly powered past the difficulties. But the nearly 2,000 feet of climbing was catching up with me, and I fought to maintain prefect attention. Part of me just wanted off.

Above the last Zig-Zag, I started the dramatic walk

across Thank God Ledge, the amazing sliver of rock that traverses an otherwise blank face a few pitches beneath the summit Visor. I could hear noises from above — dozens, perhaps hundreds of people were on top enjoying this bluebird autumn morning. But no heads peered over the edge. I was relieved no one was watching.

I walked across Thank God ledge as a matter of pride. I'd walked its 35 foot length before, but also had crawled or hand-traversed, as most everyone does. It's less than a foot wide at its narrowest, with the wall above bulging ever so slightly at midpoint. The first few steps felt casual — like strolling along a sidewalk in the sky. But once the ledge narrowed I found myself inching along with my back glued to the face, shuffling my feet and maintaining ramrod straight posture. I paused in the very middle, staring straight out, toes overhanging the ledge. I could look down and see my pack resting at the base, 1,900 feet below, but even the slightest lean out would have pitched me headfirst off the wall. I slowly shuffled on.

Thank God Ledge ends at a short squeeze chimney which guards the beginning of the final slab to the summit. I rested for a moment beneath the 90-foot slab, glanced up to see if anyone was watching (still no one), then started up.

The first few moves follow positive holds that slowly blank out up higher. I hardly noticed the first crux — a step through onto a miserly smear. The pitch follows a ten bolt ladder, and 20 feet of thin cord hung from one of the bolts — a relic, no doubt, of some aid-climbing misadventure. As the holds thinned to nothing at all, I briefly considered running the cord under my thumb, not weighting it but having it there just in case. But that felt like cheating, so I flipped the line aside and pulled into the upper crux, feeling pleased about doing things legit.

I suddenly ground to a halt. Two days earlier, this section had felt horrendous, but I figured I'd bungled the moves, fully expecting to find some better hold or sequence this time around. Now stranded in the same desperate position on the same desperate holds, I fully understood why this pitch was originally rated 5.12. I had a moment of doubt . . . or maybe panic. It was hard to tell which. Although I'd freed the pitch several times, I could remember nothing about the moves or the holds, probably because neither was really there.

An old oval biner hung from a bolt about two inches above the pathetic ripple that was my right handhold. I alternated back and forth, chalking up my right hand and then my left, switching feet on marginal smears to shake out my fatted calves. I couldn't commit to high-stepping the last dreadful right foot smear needed to snag a good hold just out of reach. In fact I'd stalled out in the most precarious position on the entire route. I considered grabbing the biner — it was right there. With one pull, I'd be up and off.

Tourists' laughter spilled over the lip — tons of people were reveling on top. I was in a very private hell. I stroked the biner several times, fighting the urge to grab it while considering the horror of sliding 2,000 feet to my death. My calves were pumped like mad. I had to do something soon; treading water was only wearing me out. I never considered downclimbing. I was going up — it was just a matter of how high — one way or another. I never wanted to be on that slab again, so I had to finish what I started, without invalidating my ascent. Finally, I compromised. I kept my hand on the pathetic ripple but straightened my right index finger, just enough for the tip of my last pad to rest on the bottom of the oval. My thought was: if my foot blows, I might snatch the biner with one finger and check my fall.

I smeared my foot high, slowly stood up, and latched the jug. I was delivered, free of my little prison, where I'd stood silently for the longest five minutes of my life.

I nearly ran up the final 5.7 slab to the summit. Twenty or more hikers sat on the edge of the precipice, silently witnessing my final charge. No yells, no pictures. Nothing. Maybe they thought I was a lost hiker. Maybe they didn't give a shit. When I mantled onto the actual top, I was met by about 100 people spread across the summit plateau, and a conga-line of others streaming up the Cable Route. People everywhere.

I was shirtless, pumped, psyched out of my mind — thrilled beyond words to have realized such a towering dream, but slightly embarrassed that I'd gotten scared on the slab. These and many other feelings raced through me. Part of me wished someone on top would acknowledge that I'd just free soloed the Northwest Face of Half Dome in two hours and fifty minutes. Tourists on both sides and behind me slowly ate their lunch. They kissed, chatted, took scenic photos. But no one said a word about any climbing. I didn't make a sound. How could I have expressed what the last three hours of my life had really been like? It was enough that I knew.

I took off my shoes and started hiking down.

SPEED TRAP (2021)

John Long
From *Ascent*

"HOW FAR'D SHE FALL?"

"Far enough to blow the helmet off her head," said Tom. "Rescue team short-roped her off the wall, and they airlifted her out. Don't see how you survive that fall, but she did — barely."

August 2017. We'd just arrived in Yosemite Valley for a video shoot, finding Tom Evans in a corner of the cafeteria, editing photos from the rescue, which he took from El Capitan Meadow using his "big gun" telephoto lens. Whoever is climbing El Capitan, Tom shoots them for his elcapreport.com ("Unique in all the World!"), highly prized by Valley cognoscenti, and which Tom updates every evening in his van.

Tom paused on a shot of the chopper in midair, the black and tan bulk of El Cap rising in the background. At the end of a rope far below the chopper, rescue ranger Brandon Lathum and climber Quinn Brett — who was strapped into the litter — dangled in space like spiders on a string.

"Speed climbing *The Nose*?" I asked.

"What else?" said Tom. He looked ill.

Word trickled in over the following days. Quinn broke four ribs, punctured a lung, and bruised her liver in the fall. She also suffered a burst fracture of her twelfth thoracic vertebra, "typically a severe spinal injury," according to her doctors. If they knew how severe, no one was saying.

Friends started a YouCaring campaign, donations streamed in from a dozen countries, but still no word on Quinn's prognosis. Two months and three operations later, while rehabbing at Doctors Medical Center in Modesto, California, Quinn started blogging:

Will I ever walk hand in hand with Max again? WALK hand in hand. BE with Max? Live a life without diapers and worrying about shitting in the middle of the night because I have no control?

WHAT THE FUCK!

This from the woman who popped handstands on gusty Patagonian summits, who ran "Rim to Rim to Rim" (45 miles, 22,000 feet elevation gain/loss) in the Grand Canyon, and stormed up dozens of Yosemite big walls, several in record time. She was a spark on the tinder of American adventuring until, during a speed climbing run on The Nose route of El Capitan, she fell 120 feet and body slammed off another flake below. Now, she was paralyzed from the belly button down.

Sometimes I am depressed, wonder if I should be here. I

can't believe that this is where I am at. I am scared. I am sorry. I am overwhelmed.

Reading these words at home in Venice Beach, California, I pushed back from my desk as a long-forgotten scene bubbled into memory. I studied the cell phone photos in Quinn's blog — the heinous road rash, the Frankenstein gash from spinal fusion surgery, and now the horror-stricken timbre of her voice, like she woke up screaming — and thought to myself, "Damn. That could have been me."

Memorial Day, 1975. Seven years before Quinn was born. Jim Bridwell, Billy Westbay (both lost from us now), and I cast off to attempt the first one-day ascent of *The Nose*, the world's most sought-after rock climb.

"Pull this off and we'll never live it down," Jim laughed as we geared up in the dark at the base of the wall. Twice that year, teams had attempted the NIAD (Nose in a Day), bonking in the upper corners, half a mile over the trees. The NIAD was a prize and we meant to get it. I tied into the rope and charged, hell-bent. I had recently turned 21.

Shortly past dawn, I pendulumed right into the Stoveleg Crack, a laser-cut slash bisecting the sweeping granite nose where the Southwest and Southeast Faces converge. The ground dropped away as pitches that normally took an hour were dispatched in minutes, a speed achieved through constant motion and placing little to no protection. Jim promised plenty of fixed nuts and pitons in the crack but I only found a few. The climbing was steep and thuggish, but secure, so it didn't matter. Going fast was all that mattered.

By 7:00 a.m., now a third of the way up the wall, I stormed up a ladder of bolts drilled into the rock, gunning for Boot Flake, a 50-foot granite scab describing a boot if you eye it dead-on from El Cap Meadow. I'd climbed *The Nose* once before and remembered the crack along the Boot's right side as secure but off-balance. I chalked up and started tomahawking my hands into the wavy fracture. The first 20 feet felt solid so I pressed on, not bothering to place protection in the crack and waste time, jamming for the shelf and bolt anchors atop the Boot. Nearly there, my left arm cramped and my hand curled into a claw. I'd meant to fully hydrate the night before but sipped on beers instead. I shook my frozen arm, my right hand creeping from a greasy hand jam.

My eyes darted down 50 feet to my last protection. When I pitched off — not if, but when — I'd ragdoll down and smash into Texas Flake, the jagged-edged atoll where Jim and Billy were moored, 100 feet below. I wasn't thinking about getting busted in half or even dying, but the shame of dreaming so big and performing so small. A pretender who should have known better.

I glanced at my jammed hand, melting from the crack. I had one big hexcentric on my rack and, when the cramp briefly released, I fumbled the nut into the crack, clipped in the rope, and slumped onto it. Cold sweat streamed down my neck as the mango-sized nut pivoted in the crack. I shook my arm out, reset the nut, and groped up the last bit to the shelf and the anchors. It was 7:20 a.m.

Billy grabbed the lead, swung left, and streaked across the "Gray Band" of diorite that girds El Capitan. Before I could catch my breath, the vortex of our speed ascent sucked me off the anchors and across the wall, blowing away my near miss on Boot Flake — behind me now, but I'd screwed up hugely and squeaked by on luck, nothing else.

Forty-three years later and I'm cringing in the Oval Room at the Fairmont Copley Plaza Hotel in Boston, Massachusetts, hearing about the fall I should have taken by the climber who took it — at the exact same place on Boot Flake.

"Tell me about the climb," asks Ashley Saupe, hosting The Sharp End podcast. I'm at the annual American Alpine Club gala and the band's all here, heroes and has-beens, spanning generations, everyone strands in a web stretching from the Oval Room to Yosemite Valley to the Himalayas and beyond.

Quinn gazes at Audrey with liquid brown eyes and says, "Last time I'd been in Yosemite with Hayden Kennedy, he'd taken a big fall off Pancake Flake halfway up *The Nose* during a speed push. And he came down and

192 | **YOSEMITE STORIES UNTOLD**

had a giant hematoma on his hamstring, and he and I sat by the river, and he soaked his leg and talked about how that felt. Like, he took a sixty-footer and was freaked out and he said, 'Quinn, I don't know why we're doing this speed climbing thing.'"

Hayden was doing what athletes always do at the thin end of the wedge: seek to break new ground. A competent team at a casual pace can climb El Cap trade routes with trepidation, but little fear for their lives. Hundreds do so every season. And dedicated climbers usually look to throw down a quick time, to confirm their skill and fitness, if only to themselves. Nobody wants to be the climbing equal of jazz great, Paul Desmond, who played his sax so slowly you could still hear his lines a decade after he passed.

Chasing record times, however, means no pausing to strategize, to place adequate protection, or drop anchor and regroup, however briefly. You simply charge, hell-bent, using your experience and instincts as collateral. Gravity never sleeps, so the potential danger is towering. It's also optional, and a throbbing rope burn can make even crushers like Hayden Kennedy wonder, *Why?* The question is part of the web, though hidden at first. As the adventures run together and seasons pass, partners, friends, and acquaintances drop into the void so abruptly that it rips holes in the web. The question lives in those holes.

The day before Quinn and Josie McKee headed up on *The Nose*, they learned that Hayden, 27, and his girlfriend, Inge Perkins, 23, had gone backcountry skiing below Imp

Peak, Montana. A hard slab avalanche plowed down a gully and buried them alive. Hayden clawed his way out, and dug for hours, but Inge was gone. That night, lost in the dark, Hayden killed himself.

"When Josie and I pulled into El Cap Meadow, the morning of our climb," says Quinn, as the podcast rolls, "I was texting my boyfriend about Hayden, struggling with his death. Josie and I were like — we'd planned on climbing *The Nose* so let's just go. So, out of habit, we put on our climbing gear and, out of habit, we walked to the base because that's what we did. Climb. Fast. Next thing you know we were going."

After the first one-day ascent in 1975, the NIAD remained an infrequent feat performed mostly by Valley locals. Nobody ever remembers the second team to do anything, so little glory accrued from repeating the NIAD. However, the experience was so huge and exhilarating that a burn up *The Nose* became "obligatory for hard men" throughout the '70s and '80s, albeit on a limited scale.

This all changed in 1990, when former pole-vaulting star, "Hollywood" Hans Florine, made speed climbing his life work, scaling El Cap nigh 200 times, setting speed records on most every route he bagged. His attention never strayed far from *The Nose*, where he shifted gears from one-day ascents, to elapsed time, turning the NIAD into a race ("the Indy 500 of speed climbing"). This, critically, gave leading climbers a prestigious world record to set and to break — forever. Now the NIAD, like the 100-meter dash, could never fall out of fashion.

Hans' closing statement came in 2014, while partnered with Alex Honnold (who later won an Oscar for *Solo*, the highest grossing documentary in history, about his no-rope ascent of El Capitan in 2018). The pair lowered *The Nose* speed record to a blazing two hours and forty-six minutes (2:46). His 2015 release, *On The Nose: A Lifelong Obsession with Yosemite's Most Iconic Climb*, was a bestseller in the outdoor industry. His record with Honnold felt beyond reach.

Women joined the hunt in the 1990s, though many felt female promise was scarcely tapped until 2011, when Libby Sauter and Chantel Astorga took down *The Nose* in 10:40 (the record had stood at 12:15 for a decade or so). Brett and Jes Meiris responded, clocking in at 10:26. Later that summer, Mayan Smith-Gobat and Chantel Astorga lowered the time to 7:26. In 2013, Smith-Gobat, partnered with Sauter, starched the route in 5:39, in 5:02 the following spring and, later that fall, set the speed record at 4:43 (surely one of the greatest and least-recognized feats in female sport).

Of the many who've climbed El Cap in a day, few had the time and inclination for the grueling prep work (years of skill-building and practice burns up a given route) required to take a run at a speed record. But for those who did, the action was fierce and dodgy. To most everyone else, speed climbing, like most all ascent, was simply another roller coaster. Fast and thrilling but at the end of the day, back on the ground and all out of breath, you ended up right where you'd started.

The morning after Quinn's accident, I drove to El Cap Meadow and found Tom behind his camera, hunkered in a little gravel clearing by a stunted pine, close by the Merced River. For all who have scaled El Capitan, the Meadow exerts a gravity that pulls you there, where climbers loiter (often around Tom, where the banter is rare and relentless) in random groups, or wander off alone and stare at the monolith. The wall is still a long way off, but at 3,000 feet high and several miles wide along the base, it feels like you can reach and touch it.

You sit there and bask in its raw basal force, recalling life up high, and the spells of dark brood when you'd wonder why you were working harder than you ever worked in your life, beating down the fear when below, there were tanned tourists to chase and beer to drink and sandy riverbanks to lounge on and do nothing — and everything. The answer plunged below you on the rock: You were climbing El Capitan.

Most of the ragged ensemble I found in the meadow had been on hand for Quinn's rescue, and the atmosphere felt grim. Brad Gobright wandered over. Twenty-nine and cool as an iceberg, Brad had climbed for twenty-one years, hiking world-class climbs across the Western States, often without a rope. A native Southern Californian, like myself, Brad also grew up clawing over the quartz monzonite domes out at Joshua Tree National Park, a high-desert destination area north of Palm Springs. The previous fall, he'd climbed *The Nose* half a dozen times with partner Jim Reynolds, and eleven more times that season, honing their game for an all-out run at the speed record. I asked Brad what he thought happened to Quinn on Boot Flake. His eyes never left El Cap. "No idea."

The man was locked in. Scanning the rock like a predator. Absorbed in a half-remembered forcefield I could feel and almost taste. Labels and limits, I recalled, stood no chance in that forcefield, which makes the game so seductive, and sparks the craving to throw all your marbles at *The Nose*. We all underestimated the heat once we had.

Brad's partner, Jim Reynolds, had said in an interview, "The closer we're getting to the record, we're pushing the boundary between dangerous and reckless just a little bit more. So we're starting to wonder: can we just take a little bit more risk and get it finished, so we don't have to come back and take all that risk again?"

Eleven days later, Brad and Jim Reynolds pulled the trigger. Gobright led from the ground to the top of Boot Flake, 1,300 feet up the wall, placing but three cams over that distance. They smoked the route in 2:19:44, breaking Honnold and Florine's record by four minutes.

In Josh Lowell's and Peter Mortimer's feature-length documentary, *The Nose Speed Record*, Honnold later said:

"When Brad and Jim did the record, at the top they had an entire sixty-meter rope between them but nothing clipped, no gear between them, and Brad was literally just holding onto the bolts with his fingers. And I'm like — what are you guys doing?!" The inference being that Alex and Hans levitated up *The Nose* on savvy and legerdemain, while Gobright and Reynolds burgled the record through recklessness. Brad, among the world's most accomplished big wall free climbers, played along because he knew better.

"Alex tells me, 'Dude! You guys are really sketchy,'" said Gobright. "I'm like, 'Yeah. It's sketchy. But that's why I got the record . . . and you don't.'"

The following fall, Gobright perished in a rappelling accident while climbing in Mexico, and Reynolds flummoxed the adventure world by climbing up and down 4,000-foot Mount Fitz Roy, in Patagonia, with no rope.

"What about your fall off Boot Flake?" asks Ashley. We're half an hour into the podcast and half the crowd looks ready to run. Quinn straightens and describes reaching the crack, and how the rope gets stuck below but there's a great loop of slack out in her lead rope, so she starts jamming out the Boot with no belay, "because that's the way you climb the pitch. Josie yells up that we're at two hours, which is, like — sick. We're on a really cruiser pace."

As Quinn nears the top of the Boot, Hayden Kennedy flashes through her mind. She gropes for a camming device, slung to her harness, which she might slot in the crack in an emergency. Like now. Except she's dropped the cam. Or maybe placed it already. She isn't sure which. Only that everything is racing south — just as it'd gone for me, and for dozens of others present who've battled critical moments and inexplicably escaped, while Quinn did not. A dreadful few among us are sole survivors, and sit still as statues as Quinn recounts the moment: feet paddling, hanging for her life on Boot Flake, fumbling gear and thinking, "'I shouldn't do that,' or, 'I shouldn't have done that.' One second of a feeling like in an elevator," says Quinn. "Then — falling. Granite whooshing before my eyes. Thankfully, I don't remember the rest."

Quinn briefly reviews the rescue operation (a more technical extraction is hard to imagine), and Ashley asks how her recovery is going.

"It's been a pile of shit," says Quinn, "and it's been amazing, with the people who've come to help me."

Audrey mentions the YouCaring fundraiser, how strangers from Kenya to Israel have given over $125,000. Quinn's game face, courageously worn so far, shatters and falls. "I did a stupid thing, and people are helping me and it's pretty amazing. So, thank you very much."

We muster smiles. Offer encouraging words. But the tension won't break till we stop our perverse well-wishing and finally sync up with Quinn, with all our dread and jagged edges. And the inexorable sundown of feeling hits home for all of us whose partners and friends have fallen through the net, leaving gaping holes, which stir with the doomed and the missing.

As the past breaks out in our hearts, the Oval Room is a house of catharsis. Scattered applause breaks the trance, and none too soon. I'll give the crisis this palliative minute, as a tribal rite. But I'm not yet ready to discover where I truly stand — about Quinn, speed climbing, any of it.

I peer at the clouds, brushed on the ceiling. Legend says that circa 1905, after John Singer Sargent finished the murals in the iconic Boston City Library across the street, he dropped by the Oval Room and painted an angel on the ceiling. I can't find it. Searching around, I find the next best thing: Libby "The Liberator" Sauter, with her bucket-full of freckles and a smile off a toothpaste ad. She's one of Quinn's partners from way back, and spent much of that first month at her bedside. Libby splits time between cutting-edge adventuring (a skilled slackliner and ultrarunner, she had concurrently held speed climbing records for *The Nose*, Salathé Wall, and Lurking Fear routes on El Capitan — the latter bagged with Quinn), and working as a war zone cardiac nurse in places like Benghazi, Libya. Libby Sauter never plays it safe.

My smile feels like a clown mask as Libby and I join the mob swarming through the exit. What is this, a celebration? A wake? By what crazy fluke are we even alive to be here, especially the alpinists and big mountain folk who dominate this crowd. Seen from the perspective of my Venezuelan-born daughter, a Latina pediatrician who donates her time to Doctors Without Borders, what gives with these callow white yahoos and their hoary legacy? What would all the dead say to our back-slapping and tequila shooters in their honor, as those left bereft ask why for the rest of their lives?

"My West Point class must have a thousand man-years of combat at this point," former soldier and Patagonia climber, Gregory Crouch, emailed me that morning, "what with Panama, Desert Storm, and all that shit in Afghanistan and Iraq, and we have one person Killed In Action. Of the people with whom I've shared the rope in my 35 years of climbing, seventeen of them are dead. It's like the Somme."

Most mountaineers venturing onto big, technical mountains have repeatedly feared for their lives — but many charge regardless. Climbing as fetish. But I'm a rock climber, where the risks are fewer. Unless you travel to stormy venues like Patagonia, in southern Argentina, talent and technology have largely brought the hazards under control, especially in pacific areas like Yosemite. To peer over the edge, a rock climber must solo or speed climb, or intentionally chase other dangers. The stated goal, as it goes for most alpinists, is to reap remarkable experiences, or perhaps, set a record, capture the public's eye, and get a sponsor. Or keep one. But every avid soloist or speed climber has, at some time, seen God.

I have a place in the hotel and Libby and Quinn will use it as a staging area before the gala dinner that evening. I let the pair into my room and lift Quinn from her chair and onto the bed. She can't weigh more than 100 pounds, her once-strong runner's legs now as slender as reeds. Her vacant eyes betray the incomprehensible disillusionment of going, in seconds, from a flower with a cannon inside, to . . . this.

Here's a conflict I can only square at the open bar downstairs. Better head over to Copley Square and the renowned Boston Public Library, a few blocks away. I'll admire Sargent's portraits, duck into a shady booth, and eyeball the pictures in *Surfer* magazine.

Libby walks me back to the elevator. We both occasionally work for the same outdoor clothing brand, but we haven't spoken in months. She's still climbing, and harder than ever, she says, but on short sport routes, bolted and secure. Nothing like her halcyon days when she set all those speed records on El Cap, including the one with Quinn. Watching a soulmate go from able-bodied to paralysis "makes speed climbing a whole lot less cool."

The last time Libby went trad climbing and got way off the ground, she visualized bodies tumbling through the air. When one of the best of them all sees this in her mind, all that giddy valorizing we sometimes ascribed to speed climbing feels bogus as Halo Jones and Spiderman.

Libby will later write in *Rock and Ice* that she had been "guilty of having spread the bullshit narrative that there is a way to speed climb safely. At my peak of speed climbing on *The Nose*, I would do fifteen pitches on ten cams for the first block and, while it 'felt safe' — it sure as shit wasn't. I'm not telling people not to speed climb, but that kind of climbing isn't for me anymore."

"That kind of climbing" involves the leader and the second climbing concurrently ("simul-climbing") on opposite ends of a sixty- or seventy-meter-long rope. Once the team goes live, it's a blood oath. If the leader falls, or the second falls and pulls off the leader, the team is saved only by whatever protection they've placed between them, rarely more than one piece, since placing gear takes time and carrying it takes energy. Any fall will likely be 100 feet or more, prompting the universal credo that "you cannot fall while speed climbing." Advanced techniques, like short-fixing (quantum mechanics is easier to explain), are faster yet sketchier still.

Fact is, belaying at an anchor (at the end of a given pitch, or rope length) is where a climber recovers, however briefly. Now it's like a boxing match with no bell between rounds, because there are no rounds. It's a slugfest start to finish. What's more, climbing so much technical rock requires holding a surgeon's focus for hours on end; but hold it you must, between the short span of our fingertips and a sloping edge, or the climb can undo your life.

Libby's cautionary drift echoed through the adventure world at large. In an interview for *The Nose Speed Record*, Gobright said, "chasing The Nose record is absolutely dangerous. There's no getting around that." In a piece for *Outside*, writer and alpinist, Kelly Cordes, no stranger to danger himself, noted that, no matter how you play it, the techniques used at hyper-speed are complex and potentially lethal, a process he likened to redlining a Ferrari on a winding mountain road without a seatbelt. "Everything's fine — unless you crash," wrote Cordes. "But to embody the physical and psychological competency to race up the most iconic wall on the planet in a couple of hours must feel like flying."

The flying metaphor struck a chord with Tommy Caldwell, Cordes' neighbor and amongst the greatest large-scale rock climbers in history, whose free ascent of the Dawn Wall on El Capitan in 2015 became a worldwide media event.

"Man, I think of the wingsuit community," Caldwell said to Cordes, "how at first people were like, 'If you only fly in these conditions, only fly in this terrain, it's actually safe.' And now, everybody knows that it's just dangerous, no matter what. I wonder if speed climbing is the same."

Not the same, but equally addictive. I half-seriously coined it the "Icarus Syndrome," in light of what happened to Hans Florine, who'd climbed El Cap 178 times, breaking The Nose speed record eight times. Yet at fifty-four years old, he still needed more. On May 3, 2018, roughly six months after Brett's podcast in Boston, Hans started up Pancake Flake, 2,000 feet up *The Nose*, during a scheduled one-day ascent. A nut blew out and he crash-landed on a ledge, breaking his left tib/fib in two places and shattering his right heel.

The indomitable Alex Honnold was terribly sorry for Hans, who he'd partnered with two years before to capture the speed record from Dean Potter and Sean Leary (both perished wingsuit flying), only for Gobright and Reynolds to snatch it away the following autumn. Now Florine had an external steel fixator bolted onto his leg and Honnold wanted his record back. He enlisted Tommy Caldwell's services a week after Florine's crash, and the two began running laps on *The Nose*, perfecting their systems and teamwork with each ascent.

"I've never been the danger dude," said Caldwell. But after a few swift burns up the Big Stone, he understood Florine's trademark refrain, that The Nose speed record "is the most badass competition there is."

The fact that it's also dangerous as hell, even for El Cap master Tommy Caldwell, struck home a few days later during another training run, when he logged a monster fall off the relatively easy Stoveleg Crack. Alex fell a half an hour later, burning his hand and losing a chunk of flesh while grabbing the rope. It could have gone far worse.

"It was at least a hundred feet," said Caldwell of his fall. "I was like: I'm still falling. *I'm still falling!*"

"Hope nobody saw that shit," said Honnold, on top of El Cap, after their ascent. "Kind of horrifying."

America had never fielded a better big wall squad than Alex Honnold and Tommy Caldwell, and yet both had broken the golden rule to *never fall* while speed climbing. This didn't auger well for setting records. But once the adrenaline washed through and they slept it off, they both put their falls behind them.

On May 28, Honnold and Caldwell clocked a "relatively casual lap" in 2:25, only six minutes off Gobright and Reynolds's record pace. Two days later, they brought it home in 2:10:15, smashing the record. Might they possibly reach the "mythical milestone" and log a sub-two-hour ascent? This meant going a full five percent faster than their quickest lap, which increased the risks exponentially.

At the velocity top speed climbers were traveling, with the margin for error so thin, and with even the best logging monster falls in the process, many felt speed climbing was a game of chance, that it was impossibly lucky that a team hadn't straight-up died. Several days later, on June 2, 2018, that all changed.

Tim Klein, 42, and Jason Wells, 45, had climbed together since their early 20s, and had nearly 200 ascents of El Cap between them, including a mind-numbing 40 one-day ascents of the Salathé Wall (the other El Cap route regularly speed climbed). Their accident occurred on the lower reaches of the Salathé, on moderate climbing above a prominent feature called the Half-Dollar, where the pair had passed another party attempting to free climb the route. No one is certain what happened, but whatever protection and anchors they had failed after the leader fell, and the partners experienced a terror no human needs to know, taking a 1,000-foot ride into the dirt.

Tim Klein and Jason Wells had no truck with record times. They simply loved climbing fast, and had more experience doing so than any team alive. But they still simul-climbed, still carried as little gear as possible, and placed it frugally. Since they intimately knew the route, and their own limits, so long as they kept their speed a hair's breadth below maximum, what did they have to fear? They'd already managed one-day ascents of the very same route approaching four dozen times. They had this.

Climbing magazine waxed that "speed climbing is the inevitable expression of our basic human yearning for transcendent experience." Maybe so, but *Climbing* had taken the dramatist's prerogative to milk the glory and skip the body count. Quinn was paralyzed, Florine was laid up in traction, and Klein and Wells were dead, both leaving wives and young children behind. The adventure world, smarting from a moral whiplash, could not so easily unpack this. Many insiders knew the fastest teams, like a conquering army, claim everything in their path. Since only elapsed time mattered, speed climbing has very narrow meaning, and could quickly become a force so misleading that even the greatest send was a pyrrhic victory. Stunning performances were happening, but gallant depictions of speed climbing sounded tone deaf.

Several weeks after the Salathé Wall tragedy, while cragging out at Joshua Tree, I ran into a young high-desert climber from the party Klein and Wells passed on the Half-Dollar. He had watched the pair hurtle past (and so close by that, fearing impact, he violently sucked himself into the wall, jamming his head onto a crack) as they cartwheeled 1,000 feet straight into the ground. A gruesome experience still haunting the climber and which, for me, knocked the shine off speed climbing forever. The effects ran deeper still, but my ostrich-like avoidance of my own feelings kept me a stranger to myself. Caldwell, being Caldwell, knew he had to get back on the horse, but he did so with few illusions.

"With all the carnage this past year," said Caldwell, "it makes me hesitate . . . a bit."

But the enormity of the two-hour barrier, and the thrill of the hunt, trumped his fear. On June 6, 2018, four days after Wells' and Klein's accident, Alex and Tommy started up *The Nose* at 6:00 a.m. and topped out 1 hour and 58 minutes later.

Kelly Cordes got hold of Honnold and Caldwell on his cellphone shortly after they reached the summit. Listening over the speakerphone, he asked Caldwell if he had designs on going even faster.

"Totally done," he said.

Tommy is only an acquaintance, but I take him at his word. Meanwhile, Honnold, floating over Yosemite's scorched earth, was looking past the "mythical milestone" and into the future, as only Honnold can. He later wrote he believes the true human potential for speed climbing El Cap is 1:30. Or even 1:15.

Two blocks down Boylston Street, the Boston Public Library heaves into view. First the red tile roof sloping into a green copper cornice, flecked with seashells and dolphins above a frieze of classical figures — winged horses, an eagle on a branch. Below this lie thirteen arched bay windows faced with wooden Roman grillwork, painted dark to appear as iron.

Soon I'm in Copley Square, gazing across at three high arches trimmed with wrought-iron lanterns, which form the library entrance. Out front, two allegorical female figures, cast in dark bronze and glistening in rainwater, sit on rusticated pedestals. One hooded figure, on behalf of Art, holds a palette and a paintbrush. The other, examining an orb in her hand, represents Science.

I sit on an icy park bench, trying to shake my funk, staring across at architect Charles Follen McKim's "palace for the people," a hulking Historic Landmark faced in pink granite, as though McKim built Boston their own El Capitan. Like Mecca, like Yosemite Valley, many come to pay homage. My eyes tilt up and I read the names chiseled in stone panels below the bay windows: Zeno, Plato, over to Praxiteles, on to Kepler and Laplace, settling on Da Vinci, Spinoza, and Bach. A board of trustees first envisioned this library in the 1860s, as a Renaissance-style monument to those who kept dreaming and getting-after until the world reimagined itself.

I'll never see my name chiseled in granite, but the getting-after has sustained me when nothing else could. And I've loved the fiery questing of it all. Having a raison d'être. Being the first human being to do *something*.

From my late teens onward, my strongest sense of meaning derived from flying close to the sun, knowing that with speed climbing and soloing, as with art, politics, and crime, it's what you get away with that counts. But every Icarus has an expiration date, and friends and family squirming on the ground, so questions lingered.

When does a competitive spirit become a reckless fling with death? When does ambition mutate into a selfish crusade for fame? There's more to the game than these thorny dichotomies. And no question, dreaming and getting-after are as tightly woven into some of us as the apocalyptic elements of life. But even the incomparable Tommy Caldwell, who heard the rattling chains, drew a chalk line on the rock and is "totally done" with speed climbing. Otherwise, danger becomes a granite-hard drug mainlined in a haunted house with no value beyond itself. There lies No Man's Land. There lies the black hole of coming back to consciousness and saying, "I can't feel my legs." But if I had it all to do over again, I would, in a heartbeat. It's a conflict I could never live without.

Quinn was barely out of rehab when *living without* became a global mandate as the coronavirus locked us down and swept 3.3 million souls off the face of the earth. The pandemic dragged on and our communal fear and neuroticism seemed to blot out the sun, as society reorganized along our fault lines. Most of us also had those take-stock moments that a crisis hand delivers; speed climbing was in nobody's thoughts. Yet as the hospitals emptied out and the world opened up once more, many realized that without challenge, life lacks carbonation. A point made clear in *The Greater Fool: Brad Gobright and the Blinding Shine of Originality*, Lucas Roman's superb biography (penned during the pandemic) of former Nose speed record holder, the late Brad Gobright.

"The Greater Fool," wrote Roman, "is the one who turns into the storm when all common sense and foot traffic points the other way. Intrepid and unwitting as they may be, they're also the ones we need."

Despite losing her husband to speed climbing, Becky Wells still says she would never tell Jason not to go to Yosemite and do what he loved. "He called El Cap the Magic Stone," she said. "It gave him what he needed to be the person he wanted to be. It fed his soul."

"Had I summited that day [of my accident]," said Quinn Brett from her wheelchair, "I would probably still be speed climbing. I mean, it's a pretty awesome feeling."

And this feeling, this experience, has little to do with records. It's a reckoning with our limits and our capacity to act with skin in the game, against all odds, on a vertical stage known as the ne plus ultra of natural magnitude. We rightfully ask why, as the sun sets over the valley, but answers give us nothing.

POSTSCRIPT

When the WHO declared a pandemic in March, 2020, speed climbing was on nobodies mind. But as the crisis slowly wound down, and climbers returned to the Valley in numbers, speed climbing — forever a niche pursuit for specialists — once again started picking up steam. The first big statement occurred on October 10, 2023, when 28-year old Nick Ehman, a Yosemite Rescue

Team member, and longtime valley crusher, soloed The Nose in a scorching 4 hours, 39 minutes, outpacing Alex Honnold's solo record, set in 2010, of 5 hours, 50 minutes.

Honnold was congratulatory, telling Climbing, "I'd love to talk to Nick about his whole experience — he must be feeling super dialed on the Nose. No one has really been playing the speed climbing game for several years; it's great to see someone getting after it again."

"Will Honnold ever make a return to take possession of his record once again?" asked Climbing, who thought it doubtful, but not impossible. "I'm not sure if I'd ever try to go faster," said Honnold. "It would take a lot of time in Yosemite and I'm just not there as much anymore. But it sure would be fun."

MAGIC MUSHROOM: A FEMALE ASCENT OF EL CAP'S SECOND-HARDEST FREE ROUTE (2017)

Barbara Zangerl

From *The American Alpine Journal*

Forty meters below the summit, what had seemed impossible had almost become reality. It was day nine on the wall, and Jacopo Larcher and I both were tired from the previous days. But our motivation was stronger than ever. The sun was shining, we were hanging out in our portaledge, and the weather was on our side. Although it was much too warm to try the next hard pitch in the sunshine, we kept getting perfect conditions at night. Waiting for sunset felt like an eternity, and our eyes keep wandering up the last big challenge of Magic Mushroom, the 5.14a "Seven Seas" pitch shortly before the top.

When we arrived in Yosemite on the 10th of October 2017, we weren't sure which route we would attempt. My big dream was to climb the Nose, while Jacopo had cast an eye on Magic Mushroom, which leads up a steep wall a bit further left. Of course I was psyched to try that as well, but when I saw the topo — there were so many hard pitches. It sounded more like an interesting long-term project. But when we looked up El Cap the first time that fall, we quickly dropped our Nose plans. It was naïve to think it would not be overcrowded at the best time of the year.

And so, Magic Mushroom. The route began with perfect splitters and beautiful, varied climbing. This continued until we reached the first hard pitch, the sixth. We immediately knew we would not be able to just "climb" that pitch, not even with the occasional rest. We had to restore missing protection and clean the cracks, sometimes for hours, before we could attempt to redpoint. Our chosen style of climbing was ground up, without checking out pitches from above. This took a lot of time, as there is hardly any fixed protection in the route and we had little aid climbing experience — this was equally adventurous and thrilling, and we had to fight hard for every pitch. After another eight days on the wall, we finally made it to the top, our first milestone, but still far from any serious bid to free climb the whole route.

After that we invested more days working on the crux pitches, spending quite a lot of time on the last hard 5.14a pitch before the top, which turned out to be the most difficult for me. (Not so for Jacopo, who found his personal crux on pitch 20.) I was able to climb all the sequences of the Seven Seas, but hooking it all up in one go seemed impossible. My optimism quickly dwindled. In addition, our time was running out. We had already changed our flights, but we only had two weeks left, meaning we'd only get a single chance at a continuous free push. We both wanted to lead all the pitches harder than 5.12+, which would take additional time. We had stashed food and water during our previous tries, so we would be able to stay on the wall for 12 days.

On November 30, the alarm rang at 4:00 a.m. and off we went, climbing the first pitches in darkness. Many of the lower pitches were wet, and it was mainly luck that kept us from slipping off the holds of the first 8a pitch, but then it got better. We finally arrived at Mammoth Terraces exhausted. After some quick binge-eating there was silence and we fell asleep under a clear sky.

The next morning, I felt as if I had been run over by a train. It took a lot of effort to get out of the sleeping bag and put on my climbing shoes. Hauling the bags after each lead felt like an enormous feat, costing us half an hour per pitch. It was a battle, but we finally made it to our portaledge below pitch 20 at midnight. I felt really ill, and after two spoons of rice and a cup of tea it got worse. It was quickly clear the next day would be a rest day.

After the rest I was still weak, but as I climbed the first meters above the ledge, I realized that my head felt free. No matter how this day would end, I felt relieved to be climbing at all, and this feeling took away all the pressure. Unfortunately, the day did not go that well for Jacopo — he kept slipping off the bad footholds on pitch 20 (8a+/5.13c), and he had to wait until the next day to redpoint. We still did the following 8b pitch in the evening, with Jacopo climbing the hard layback crux totally unimpressed by his previous battle.

The next day, the first 5.14a pitch waited for us. I felt recovered and fresh, and everything went smoothly. But pitch 26, which was rated 5.11, one of the easiest on the route, was soaking wet. We brushed silly amounts of chalk onto the holds and removed big soggy patches of moss — not a typical rest day! In the morning it was still completely wet, but we fought our way up, jamming wet hands and slipping off the moist footholds, relieved to know it was behind us.

Above was the Seven Seas, my personal nightmare. When we arrived it was still too hot to try this overhanging endurance monster, so we waited for evening. My first try immediately confirmed my concerns: I still was not able to maintain body tension and kept slipping off. I kept trying and trying, hoping it would start to feel easier at some point, but it didn't.

Jacopo saved that evening by fighting his way to the belay totally pumped. I felt very happy for him, but at the same time disappointed about my failure. Giving in was not yet an option. Half an hour later, the same story, again. I could not hold back my emotions and cursed and swore for at least ten minutes before I regained my composure. I knew I was too tired for another attempt, but my head wouldn't let me give in without looking yet again. And it was my head, indeed, that finally became the key! Pressing my skull against the protruding left side of the crack, under my elbow, enabled me to statically reach the crucial smeary foothold. After another rest day, I managed to climb the Seven Seas, and our cries of joy echoed from El Capitan in the first light of morning.

Barbara "Babsi" Zangerl from Austria is the only woman to free climb Magic Mushroom (VI 5.14a), generally considered the second-hardest free route on El Capitan, after the Dawn Wall. In 2019, she free climbed the Nose, her fifth El Cap free route.

EL NIÑO VIA PINEAPPLE EXPRESS — GROUND UP. FREE.

Amity Warme (2024)

The odds were never in our favor. And yet, we persevered.

The Route.

El Niño (5.13c, 25 pitches) is an adventurous route on the right side of El Capitan. Stacked with difficulty. Six pitches of 5.13 and seven pitches of 5.12. Requires a full repertoire of skills: technical face climbing, steep roof pulling, thuggy compression bouldering, and delicate slab dancing. Airy runouts, high exposure, and loose rock scattered between many five-star pitches make it a full value adventure and a big step up in difficulty and intensity from the more well-traveled routes on the left side of El Cap.

I've climbed several other big walls, but El Niño is the most difficult I've ever tried. Daunting. Intriguing. Intimidating. Inspiring. El Niño is all of these things to me. I've earned my place here. I've honed my craft, have the necessary experience, and am ready for this challenge. And yet . . . and yet we're questing into the unknown where the outcome is uncertain. This fills me with apprehension and a tantalizing desire to dive headlong into what may come. It's a strange juxtaposition of emotions, but this journey to test my limits drives me forward.

Going into the mission, we knew there would be many difficulties beyond the climbing. Some challenges were known beforehand. Others were unforeseen and spontaneously arose on the wall. Most significantly, I badly injured my finger a few days before arriving in Yosemite, but due to several factors, including my ridiculously high pain tolerance, the injury went undiagnosed. We later found out that I free climbed the entire route with a fully ruptured A2 pulley in my middle finger. Also taxing were multiple stormy nights on the wall, a soaking wet crux pitch at the top of the route, and hauling seven days' worth of supplies, plus all the tech gear, for a videographer who documented our entire adventure.

I'm feeling, excitement, nerves, awe, determination, as I return to Yosemite and survey the massive granite walls rising up around me. My whole being tingles with anticipation as I imagine myself mid-way up El Cap, staring down a crux, or waking up on my portaledge. I've arrived with big dreams but concern about my finger injury overwhelms me with self-doubt, sapping my stoke and confidence. I'm eager for the challenge overhead, grateful for the partnership and support around me, but I've always been loath to 'fail' — to miss the mark, to fall short of a goal. My mind hangs tenuously between hope and dread. My only solution is to charge and try and unpack this on the wall. There's no guarantees. None. For any of this.

My partner, Brent Barghahn, and I both set goals of free climbing the route in one continuous, ground-up push, only possible with top notch tactics and strategy. Three of the crux pitches (Black Dike, Missing Link, and Galapagos) come back-to-back-to-back, one pitch off the ground, so we decided to dial them in before committing to the full push. These first three 5.13s feature thin, technical face climbing mostly protected by generously spaced-out bolts. Read: run-outs required. Just stringing up the rope felt like a quest! My finger injury slowed us down, but through projecting these pitches, we hoped to gain the knowledge and confidence to send them and start our push up the wall.

Oh no. I've been holding out hope about my finger, but after a few days sessioning on these low crux pitches, something is clearly and deeply wrong. I was unclear about the severity of my finger injury, so I pressed onward, battling excruciating pain. 'You're tough, Amity. You can do this, hang in there . . .' I coaxed myself to believe I could still tic this project. These pitches should be well within my ability, but right now they feel impossible. My self-doubt grows but I keep willing myself to believe. The push and pull is exhausting. I have to go all in, 100% committed, to give myself a chance.

El Niño gets a ton of direct sunlight, especially in the fall, so is was tricky to time our climbing with the best conditions. On day one, we waited until evening to start climbing, to enjoy shade for the first three 5.13 pitches. Thankfully, we both made quick work of sending all three and only had to climb by headlamp on the last lead.

I am overwhelmed with relief to clip the anchor on the last of these initial crux pitches. A couple days ago I thought I'd have to bail on this whole project, and now we've both sent the first three cruxes. I feel a spark of confidence, which fills me with hope. I know it's far from over but tonight, at least, I can rest easy.

The next morning, we climbed and hauled the remaining pitches to Big Sur ledge. Then, we started working on the hardest pitch — La Niña. This pitch originally went at 5.13b/c but after several holds crumbled during previous ascents, it's a bit harder now. Brent made an impressive second-go send of this crux (while fighting bad humidity) but it took me several more goes to sort out the perfect body positions for the tenuous crux boulder sequence, especially grim with my injured finger. I then waited, impatiently, the entire day, for evening shade, only to have it start snowing the second I chalked up for the redpoint. I waited out the snowstorm, then sought to take advantage of the COLD rock. My hands numbed out on the 5.13a intro moves, but I kept it together as I entered the crux. A foot slip sent me sailing.

No. No, no, no. That was it. That was so close. But not good enough. My mind quickly jumps to, 'I'm not good enough.' A thought, a belief I know by heart. I've always been driven, self-motivated, hard-working, and focused. I live each day with a sense of urgency, a need to do all that I can with the time that I have. This mindset pushes me to make the most of every day; but it also fosters a sense of never being good enough. Of always needing to try harder, achieve more, look prettier . . . an endless list, to be sure. But I can't dwell on this right now. I have a job to do.

I lowered to the belay, rested briefly, then started up again. It was now or never — this would be my last shot to send the pitch before we had to move on. The pressure was immense but I focused, and channeled all my effort into a hard fought send. Four of six cruxes down, two more, plus lots of 5.12, to go. But now we could move onward and upward!

I am elated and relieved after sending La Niña — the hardest pitch of the entire route. Plenty of difficulties still lie ahead, but this was a big step. My finger is swollen, sore, and clearly not getting better, but the dream is still alive, and my confidence is building.

After we both sent the La Niña pitch, we quested through three more pitches of adventurous 5.12, managing to onsight all of them, and arrived at the fifth crux. The Black Cave goes at 5.13b and was the burliest of the cruxes so far — requiring more bicep power than finesse. After a couple tries to dial in the beta, we both led it cleanly the next morning, then climbed and hauled camp to the next natural bivy ledge — the Cyclops Eye.

Relief, joy, stoke, exhaustion. The past 5 days of toiling on the wall — hauling, weathering storms, managing my injury, and climbing hard day after day, is taking a toll on me mentally and physically. My muscles are aching, my hands are scraped and sore, and I'm worried sick about my finger; but we're both still sending and reveling in the thrill of pushing ourselves to the limit. It's not over, but we've surmounted every obstacle so far, and we're committed to seeing it through.

The next day, we swung leads on a few more pitches

of wild 5.12 which brought us to the final 5.13 pitch — a steep compression boulder problem. To our dismay, it was SOAKED. After throwing down several rapid fire attempts, we'd both done all the moves, but linking them with dripping wet hands felt unlikely. We returned to our bivy discouraged and exhausted, and spent the night brainstorming options. All our time, energy, and effort on this route came down to a body length of wet rock. It felt crushing to get stymied with only a few wet holds between us and a successful send. We had to find a way! Next morning we stopped up part of the seepage with a sock, and lined one of the wet holds with a scrap of tin foil. Not perfect, but enough. We were both exhausted from the past seven days of venturing through the unknown, but we dug deep and both managed to send in a style that made us proud.

This final obstacle threatened to derail our mission, but we are tough, gritty, determined people and we found a means to succeed. I wasn't willing to come this far and not put up a fight. It's hard to sit in the tension of the unknown — unsure whether or not I am capable of achieving my goal. But big wall climbing, if nothing else, is all about riding out the roller coaster of highs and lows. Hanging in there even when all the odds are against you.

THE REFLECTION:

I find big wall climbing compelling because you need bouldering power coupled with sport climbing endurance, all in tandem with high level trad climbing expertise. And the head to stay with the process. In addition to climbing well day after day, you need the physical stamina to haul heavy loads and the logistical prowess to problem solve when things inevitably go awry. Mental toughness, performing under pressure while tired, hungry, hot or cold, stiff, sore, etc. are all part of the gambit. And on top of all that you must string together one of the best climbing performances of your life, hour after hour, day after day. There's no coming back next week when you feel better because time, energy, and limited resources requiring careful management. To me, questing into the unknown and overcoming those obstacles is the allure and the magic of big wall climbing. El Niño challenged me both mentally and physically — as any difficult undertaking does. I'm grateful for a place like Yosemite where the natural magnitude inspires me to continue seeking new adventures, pushing my limits, and honing my craft, following the footsteps of those who have paved the way before me.

ABOUT THE PUBLISHER

Di Angelo Publications was founded in 2008 by Sequoia Schmidt—at the age of seventeen. The modernized publishing firm's creative headquarters is in Los Angeles, California, with its distribution center located in Twin Falls, Idaho. In 2020, Di Angelo Publications made a conscious decision to move all printing and production for domestic distribution of its books to the United States. The firm is comprised of eleven imprints, and the featured imprint, Catharsis, was inspired by Schmidt's love of extreme sports, travel, and adventure stories.

www.ingramcontent.com/pod-product-compliance
Lightning Source LLC
Jackson TN
JSHW020139210525
84562JS00001B/1/J